Stolen Generations

Stolen Generations

Survivors of the Indian Adoption Projects and 60s Scoop

Trace L. Hentz

Blue Hand Books
Greenfield, MA

Adoption Biography/Anthology/American Indian History

Stolen Generations: Survivors of the Indian Adoption Projects and 60s Scoop

(BOOK THREE: Lost Children of the Indian Adoption Projects)

© 2016 Trace L Hentz

Library of Congress: On File

Hentz, Trace L. [1956-]

ISBN-13: 978-0692615560 (Blue Hand Books)

Kindle Ebook

First Edition

Book Cover Artist Terry Niska Watson (White Earth) Design: Blue Hand Books | Formatting and Pre-Press: PressBooks

All Photos: (by permission of participants in book)

Publisher: Blue Hand Books, 442 Main St. #1061, Greenfield, MA 01301

Published in the United States

Contents

All proceeds from ebook sales will benefit Levi EagleFeather's Iron Eagle Feather Project.

Email for more information: laratrace@outlook.com

Once Upon A Time

Johnathan Brooks (Northern Cheyenne)

Once upon a time in North America, The First People, Indians in their particular tribes, were looked upon as savages by the people who invaded their country. The savages were thought to be an impediment to progress, so their Governments decided to take their children away, and to change them and erasing their languages, their customs and their culture. The leaders in Canada and America built residential boarding schools and orphanages and filled them with these children while some children were taken for adoption. I was one of those children.

As a child, being Indian was slightly confusing since my adopted parents in England, far from any other Native Americans, raised me. My adopted mother told me when I was six, when I was watching a Western movie with cowboys and Indians, what I was, but this did not tell me who I was. What had happened to me or why I was placed into adoption, was a mystery for many years until I returned to Montana a young man where finding answers meant finding my relatives on my Northern Cheyenne reservation.

In the book, *TWO WORLDS: Lost Children of the Indian Adoption Projects*, I told my story. I explained how I found both of my biological parents who did want to give me a better life. The sad truth was, many desperately poor Indian parents felt they had no choice but to let their children go to new parents.

Records show that, one quarter of all Indian children were placed in adoptive homes or orphanages, and by 1969 eighty-five percent of the Indian children in sixteen states in America were placed with white parents.

I am one of the fortunate ones. I have come to accept that it was my *soul* choice to experience Two Worlds for the learning that the experience has offered me through my personality. But, as for so many others, adoption was wounding, confusing, and for a long time disempowering.

For me to grow, I needed to drop any idea of being specially selected as a child victim of discrimination. Specialness can create a feeling of having been wronged, which is only an illusion or a judgment of the personality. Everyone has a basic wound, and it is those of us who understand this, who have the choice to become healers or the wounds of our brothers and sisters from different cultures, as well as our own.

What an opportunity we LOST ONES have for changing the world.

**"LIFE IS NOT MEANINGFUL UNLESS IT IS
SERVING AN END BEYOND ITSELF,**

UNLESS IT IS OF VALUE TO SOMEONE ELSE"

–ABRAHAM JOSHUA HESCHEL

Suggested reading:

The Shift—by Dr Wayne W. Dyer

Johnathan Brooks (Northern Cheyenne) lives in Tunbridge Wells, England. He contributed to the anthologies TWO WORLDS and CALLED HOME. His website:

www.spiritbearcoaching.com, January 2016

Preface

Trace Lara Hentz (editor)

It's about the land.

It's about taking the land.

No matter how. No matter what.

Our parents and grandparents (and their parents) lost territorial land and their children…*

We adoptees, the stolen generation.

We are <u>all</u> collateral damage.

We were never expected to survive.

I'm not sure we did.

*Boarding Schools removed three or more generations from their tribal families.

A 60s Scoop Adoptee on Facebook asked recently, "How do I heal this?"

OUR HISTORY

"The history books are awash with the atrocities leveled against the Indigenous peoples of North America since European settlers first arrived on this continent in the 15th century. Despite this consensus among historians, the United States federal government has never formally acknowledged how its policies directly led to the near eradication of the Native inhabitants of this land. A formal acknowledgement needs to occur. Healing for all parties begins with the truth."
—Chase Iron Eyes, attorney for the Lakota People's Law Project

"They are committing the greatest indignity human beings can inflict on one another: telling people who have suffered excruciating pain and loss that their pain and loss were illusions." —Elie Wiesel, *Night*

...Shannon Smith, executive director of the ICWA Law Center in Minneapolis, explained that the Indian Child Welfare Act federal law was created in the wake of devastating "kill the Indian, save the child" practices designed to "educate the Indian out of a child."

"If you could remove children from families, they would be better off, have a better way of life, [and] a better future. Not only were Native American kids losing their language, customs, and cultural heritage, but tribes were losing their future members. By 1978, tribes recognized these practices were destroying the ability of tribes to continue to exist." [http://thinkprogress.org/justice/2016/04/08/3754462/indian-child-welfare-act-case-goldwater/]

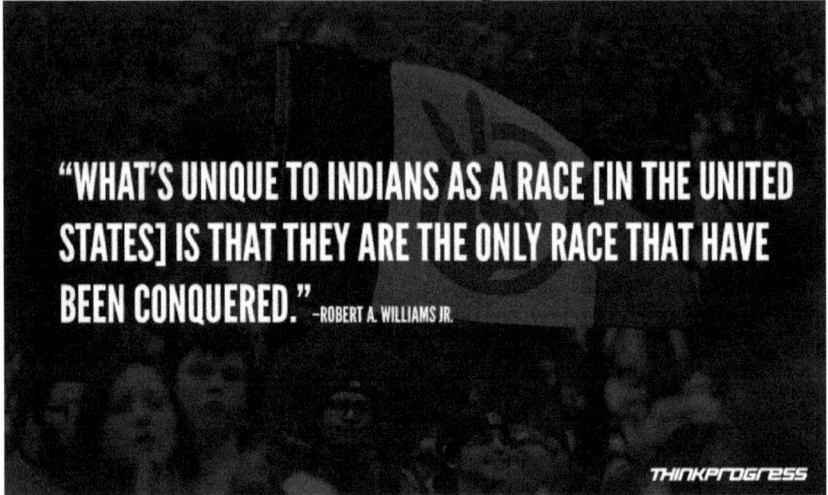

"WHAT'S UNIQUE TO INDIANS AS A RACE [IN THE UNITED STATES] IS THAT THEY ARE THE ONLY RACE THAT HAVE BEEN CONQUERED." -ROBERT A. WILLIAMS JR.

THINKPROGRESS

...It was for this reason the Department of Indian Affairs in Canada and the Bureau of Indian Affairs, in the United States, shared ideas about the eradication of Indigenous minds through the effective use of the residential schools for the purpose of assimilating Indigenous peoples by way of attack on the fundamental base of the knowledge systems and their realities, their languages.

One residential school survivor tells her story through her children's storybook. She states,

> We were told what time to get up, what time to eat, when to pray and when to go to the bathroom. Everything was timed; everything was regulated, and I realize that during that process they had stolen my will...my will to do anything and my freedom of choice in all matters.

If we didn't do what we were told they'd take you to the principal's office and they'd pull down your pants and give it to you on your bare ass. Also during this process, we weren't allowed to speak our language and we were taught nothing about our traditional ways, or our heritage or anything about our culture… (Harper, 1993, p. 3).

Since the inception of residential schools in Canada, Indigenous people have suffered a serious blow to our communities and our ways of life, the most prominent loss being the loss of our languages. Taiaiake Alfred states in his book, *Peace, Power and Righteousness,* "Our bodies may live without our languages, lands, or freedom, but they will be hollow shells. Even if we survive as individuals, we will no longer be what we Rotinonhsyonni call *Onkwehonwe*—the real and original people—because the communities that make us true indigenous people will have been lost." (Alfred, 1999, p. xv).

My parents who adopted me had no idea I was stolen," said Nina Segalowitz, a child of what's known as the 60s Scoop. "They had no idea the scope of how many kids…had been stolen and were in the system." Segalowitz grew up in Montreal, the daughter of a white Jewish father and a Filipino mother. But she was born Anne-Marie Thrasher, in Fort Smith, Northwest Territories. LINK: http://www.cbc.ca/beta/news/canada/montreal/real-talk-on-race-sixties-scoop-not-recognized-1.3494343

Telling our stories is a critical piece to healing the trauma of Indigenous adoption and so, as an adoptee, it is important to be both a teller and someone who "bears witness" to the stories of others. Although I am happy to be closing the door on telling mine, there are so many stories yet to be told.—Raven Sinclair, LAND OF GAZILLION ADOPTEES

"Storytelling is an important aspect of Ojibwe culture. My ability to tell a good tale can be used as a tool for teaching and connecting. Even though I grew up outside of my Native community and culture, my stories helped me to become a part of the community that I had lost. Adoption is part of the contemporary tales that Native people need to tell…" —Tamara Buffalo, published author-poet-visual artist

One by one, as the years pass me by, I still find it so amazing that the grief and trauma that I still carry from being separated at birth from my mother continues to follow me around and exposes itself at the most inconvenient times. I feel like my heart and spirit is that of a gypsy where although I physically stay in one place, my soul keeps wandering around searching and gets so lost. I often stuff it back into its compartment but at times it just creeps out with no warning and slaps me upside the head and I am forced to confront the emotions time and time again. I don't know that I will ever actually organize this all within myself and find a place of comfort and peace with it all." —Janey Martin Hart, Red Lake Ojibwe Split Feather Adoptee, 2011

Scott LaVergne left a comment on "American Indian Adoptees": Thank you. I am a father who lost his daughter to this insidious practices of welfare. Thank you for exposing its underbelly. I think great shame should exist for all those parents who make a child live secrets. We are all learn or should know secrets are tantamount to lies, corruption. I am angry my daughter has grown up to support the people that raised her in secret and what they care about is that their family not get broken up? Wow, wow, wow? wtf eh? Who the hell are they kidding? Apparently my daughter has bought into it, she carries a picture of the welfare lady who played the cruelest role in this whole mess smiling her ass off in the hand-off. What's worse they (the adoptive family, including my daughter) have idealized that moment. She knows she is a lost bird herself now. I am so angry how systematically mothers are taken advantage of...encouragement, not discouragement, to keep their own child.

"The child is everything. They're the gift from the creator. They are life. They are the ones who are going to sustain the tribe." —Loa Porter, Ho Chunk Nation adoptee and elder, Missing Threads documentary

It's not just about removing children, it's dismantling every aspect of their being in the process. —gkisedtanamoogk, First Light Film

Media coverage accounted for the large impact of the [Indian Adoption] project. It induced white couples to adopt Native children.

...Indian Adoption Project Director Arnold Lyslo listed the main newspaper articles which contributed to stimulate the desire of white couples to adopt a Native child. [For example,] Arlene Gilberman's article, "My forty-five Indian godchildren" issued in the review, *Good Housekeeping*. Eight hundred couples favourably responded to it. Other articles such as "God forgotten Children," "Indian children find homes" and "Interracial Adoption" also encouraged white couples to adopt a Native child. —Claire Palmiste ["From the Indian Adoption Project to the Indian Child Welfare Act: the resistance of Native American communities," *Indigenous Policy Journal Vol. XXII, No. 1 (Summer 2011)*.]

It is also worth noting how overall spikes in suicide prevalence found in Indigenous communities around the world indicate a strong correlation with the socio-political marginalization brought on by colonization. In other words, the suicide epidemic—which is at heart a crisis of mental health—is directly related to, if not directly caused by, the loss of culture and identity set in motion by colonialism. Cultural continuity—and perhaps most specifically, native language preservation and retention—plays a crucial role in overcoming the ongoing native suicide epidemic—and indeed near universal barriers to indigenous mental health—once and for all First Nations, on a community by community basis.
—*Courtney Parker and John Ahni Schertow / Intercontinental Cry*

...SCARS ARE SOUVENIRS YOU NEVER LOSE...
-GOO GOO DOLLS LYRICS

my deepest thanks to the contributors, filmmakers, historians… and for the children living and dead, past, present and future…

"Zintkala Nuni never gave up hope that one day she would find out where she really belonged." —Renee Samson Flood

Zintkala Nuni, Lost Bird of Wounded Knee —a Lakota child survived the Wounded Knee massacre (Dec. 29, 1890) and was adopted by a prominent white couple… only to endure a life of racism, abuse and poverty. She died at age 29. Her poignant story is told in "Lost Bird of Wounded Knee." (SD PBS)

Editor's Note

A wave of historic discovery: THANKS to academic author Margaret D. Jacobs' latest book "A GENERATION REMOVED: THE FOSTERING AND ADOPTION OF INDIGENOUS CHILDREN IN THE POSTWAR WORLD." I have told many people this could help with a class action lawsuit for America's Stolen Generations.

About her book: On June 25, 2013, the U.S. Supreme Court heard the case *Adoptive Couple vs. Baby Girl*, which pitted adoptive parents Matt and Melanie Capobianco against baby Veronica's biological father, Dusten Brown, a citizen of the Cherokee Nation of Oklahoma. Veronica's biological mother had relinquished her for adoption to the Capobiancos without Brown's consent. Although Brown regained custody of his daughter using the Indian Child Welfare Act (ICWA) of 1978, the Supreme Court ruled in favor of the Capobiancos, rejecting the purpose of the ICWA and ignoring the long history of removing Indigenous children from their families.

In *A Generation Removed*, a powerful blend of history and family stories, award-winning historian Margaret D. Jacobs examines how government authorities in the post–World War II era removed thousands of American Indian children from their families and placed them in non-Indian foster or adoptive families. By the late 1960s an estimated 25 to 35 percent of Indian children had been separated from their families.

Jacobs also reveals the global dimensions of the phenomenon: These practices undermined Indigenous families and their communities in Canada and Australia as well. Jacobs recounts both the trauma and resilience of Indigenous families as they struggled to reclaim the care of their children, leading to the ICWA in the United States and to national investigations, landmark apologies, and redress in Australia and Canada.

Editor's Note: I met Margaret at Yale at a conference in 2014. She has mentioned the anthology *Two Worlds* in her new book. I thanked her for all her work, and the research in her books. She helped us Lost Children. We hugged. We both cried.

[Photo: Craig Chandler/University Communications/
University of Nebraska-Lincoln. Margaret Jacobs, professor of
history and director of the Women's and Gender Studies
Program at the University of Nebraska, Lincoln, has just
published a second volume based on her research.]

STEALING CHILDREN: A LOOK AT INDIGENOUS CHILD REMOVAL POLICIES

Tanya H. Lee | 11/21/14 | Indian Country Today Media Network

Margaret Jacobs, professor of history and director of the Women's and Gender Studies Program at the University of Nebraska, Lincoln, won the Bancroft Prize for her book *White Mother to a Dark Race*, an investigation of the U.S. and Australian policies of breaking up indigenous families and removing children to be raised in boarding schools run by whites. She has just published a second volume based on her research. *A Generation Removed* looks at indigenous child removal policies from just after World War II up until passage of the Indian Child Welfare Act in 1978.

ICTMN interviewed Jacobs about her work. "When I got to Australia [to begin research] it was shortly after the 'Bringing them home' report [1997] had come out about the stolen generation [of Australian Aborigine children]. When I went to the archives, I asked, 'What were white women doing about indigenous children? Were they involved in this policy of the stolen generation?'"

Coming back to the U.S., she asked the same question and found that "many white women were involved in even a more pronounced manner in the United States than in Australia. They were involved in creating policy and were even hired by the federal government to carry out the policy of removing indigenous children."

"So that was the book that I wrote. It was called *White Mother to a Dark Race: Settler Colonialism, Maternalism, and the Removal of Indigenous Children in the American West and Australia, 1880-1940*. As I was researching that book I was also very interested in looking at more recent examples of the removal of indigenous children. This second book, called *A Generation Removed: The Fostering and Adoption of Indigenous Children in the Postwar World*, focuses less on white women and much more on indigenous women's experience of having children removed and the activism that they engaged in to reclaim the care of their children."

Jacobs found that during the termination period, the Bureau of Indian Affairs was eager to close down the boarding schools because they were not accomplishing the goal of assimilating American Indian children into the mainstream culture, and they were expensive. "So they turned to this policy of trying to close down the boarding schools and they turned toward a policy of trying to turn over the education and care of Indian children to the states," says Jacobs.

SOURCE: http://indiancountrytodaymedianetwork.com/2014/11/21/stealing-children-look-indigenous-child-removal-policies-157884

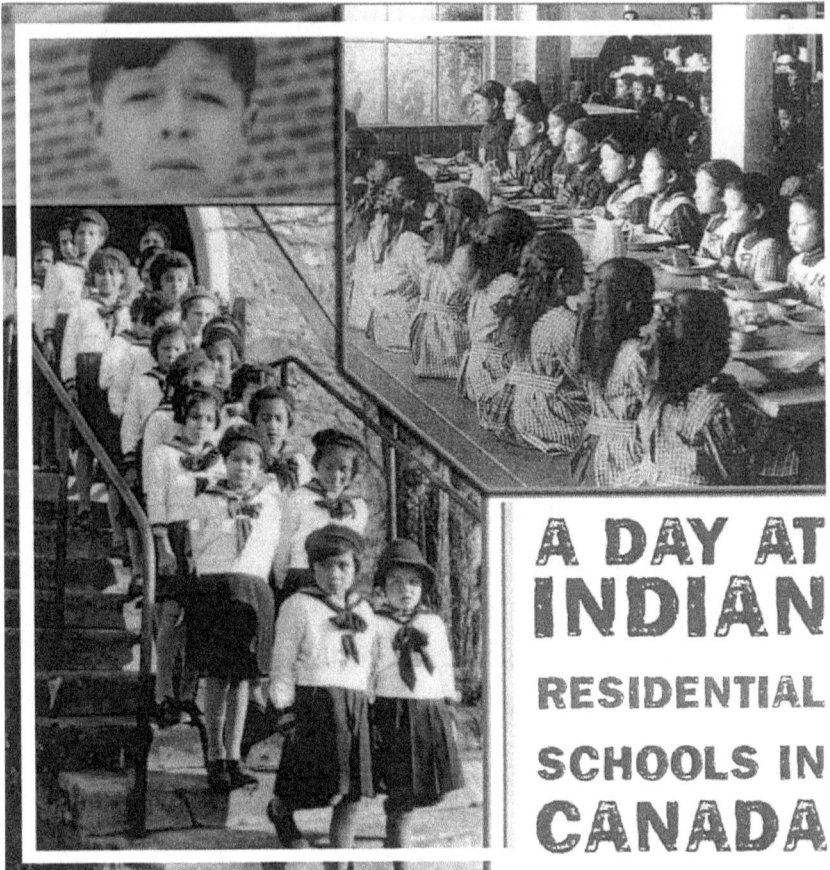

A DAY AT INDIAN RESIDENTIAL SCHOOLS IN CANADA

"The eradication of Indigenous languages was an attempt by colonial governments to eradicate the Indigenous mind, which would result in the disappearance of Indigenous knowledge for the purpose of assimilation, an act of cultural genocide." —Caroline VanEvery-Lefort READ: http://www.realpeoplesmedia.org/news/2016/1/4

Dr. Evelyn Blanchard is a member of the Laguna Pueblo of New Mexico and has been working in the field of Indian child welfare for over 50 years. A grandmother and tribal elder, Blanchard was one of the first Indian women in the country to earn a doctorate and has worked with tribes across the U.S. and Canada to establish and codify their child welfare laws. Additionally, she has worked with several states to implement best practices in the promulgation of ICWA. Read more at http://indiancountrytodaymedianetwork.com/2015/05/21/ war-words-icwa-hearings-reignite-ancient-clash-over-indian-children-part-1-160454

HISTORIC in the USA:
Almost four years ago, five Wabanaki Chiefs and Maine Governor Paul

LePage signed a mandate to launch a Maine Wabanaki-State Child Welfare Truth and Reconciliation Commission. The commission was charged with examining Maine's child welfare practices on Wabanaki people. Its focus was on "truth, healing, and change." Over the next three years, the commission collected statements from nearly 160 individuals and focus groups. A final report with findings and recommendations for future action was published on June 14, 2015. At the conclusion of its work, the commission transferred its extensive archives to the Bowdoin College Library's George J. Mitchell Department of Special Collections & Archives. The collection includes video, audio, and written statements, and other personal documents contributed by participants. It also includes founding documents, the final report, and administrative and research records. A website provides online access to all the unrestricted statements in the collection. Researchers interested in consulting other components of the collection may do so by contacting the George J. Mitchell Department of Special Collections & Archives. http://digitalcommons.bowdoin.edu/maine-wabanaki-trc/

Maine is the only state with a commission. We wait for more.

Please read Suzette Brewer (Cherokee) at Indian Country Today Media Network for the latest developments on ICWA and adoption news.

1

Born Cree in Saskatchewan, I grew up in a very different world

Nakuset (Cree)

Nakuset

I needed a baby picture for my Bat mitzvah party. The plan was to blow it up to 18 inches by 24 inches and all my friends could write messages on it.

But I didn't have any baby pictures.

The earliest photograph I had was the photo used during my adoption (above).

My parents chose me out of a catalogue of First Nations children. My adoptive parents went to Jewish Family Services, wanting to adopt a child. It was the trend in 1970, to offer First Nations children to non-Aboriginal homes.

A government-imposed initiative which has become known as "the 60s Scoop."

The solution to the enduring "Indian problem."

After the residential schools began to close down, the government began a provincial assimilation process as opposed to federal. In the late 1950's they began sending social workers into the reservations to "evaluate" if Aboriginal parents were able to bring up their children. These children were then put into the foster care system or adopted out.

It was really difficult growing up in a culture that didn't match your own. I was almost 3 years old when I was adopted.

Old enough to know that this was not my home. Cautiously waiting to see if I would be moved again.

The fact that I didn't resemble any members of my adoptive family weighed heavily on me.

I so desperately wanted to belong. Outsiders would always question why I looked so different.

It didn't help that the adoption agency advised my parents to erase my roots.

Change her name. Don't tell her she's native. Immerse her into the Jewish culture.

So, my parents, trying to be helpful, said, "When people ask why you look different, tell them you are Israeli."

I passed on that advice.

I was proud of being Native. I told everyone I was. I was hungry for my culture and looked for it everywhere.

Nakuset grew up in Jewish culture, going to synagogue, Hebrew school and Jewish summer camps. (Submitted by Nakuset)

This was not an easy task. So I chose to wear Cherokee jeans, because their logo had an Indian head dress. I watched the beach-combers so I could watch the native character Jesse. Even stared longingly at the Manitoba flag that has the buffalo head. Knowing that's where my people are from.

I think my parents had good intentions and were trying to "save me." There is such misinformation about First Nations people. When

I asked about my culture, I would often get often negative responses. For instance:

"WHEN YOU GO TO A JEWISH HOME, YOU WILL FIND LOTS OF FOOD ON THEIR TABLE. WHEN YOU GO TO AN INDIAN HOME, YOU WILL FIND DRUGS AND ALCOHOL."

"NATIVE PEOPLE ARE THE DREGS OF SOCIETY."

"IF YOU RETURNED TO YOUR RESERVATION, THEY WOULD BE SO JEALOUS THAT YOU BROUGHT UP IN A WEALTHY HOME. THE GIRLS WOULD BEAT YOU UP AND THE BOYS WOULD RAPE YOU."

"IF YOU'RE NOT CAREFUL, YOU WILL END UP A DRUG ADDICT AND A PROSTITUTE, LIKE SO MANY OF YOUR PEOPLE."

Their version of reverse psychology. Not helpful. I felt ashamed.

I was so confused. Although I had a great appreciation for the Jewish culture, as my parents brought me to synagogue, put me in Hebrew school and Jewish summer camps, I struggled to fit in.

I moved out when I became of age. It took me a couple of years to then find my way to Native Friendship Center of Montreal (NFCM). But when I did, I felt welcomed. Plus, I met all kinds of Jewish Indians. To share the same lived experience was awesome. I no longer felt alone.

The NFCM helped me regain my Indian Status. I was able to attend university. I got a B.A. in human relations. My goal was to work with the urban Aboriginal community. I started working at the Native Women's Shelter of Montreal, where I am currently the Executive Director. I'm also the co-chair of the Montreal Urban Aboriginal Community Strategy Network. I work with all different organizations and government agencies to help improve the lives of urban Aboriginals.

I often wonder how I got here.

A huge reason for my success is my Bubbi (Yiddish for grand-mother). She always believed in me. Even though I didn't believe in myself. She predicted I would do great things one day. I told her that I was probably going to jail.

If I am a good person today, it is to her benefit.

Although my childhood was challenging, I am extremely grateful for the experience.

It made me who I am today.

Pierre Tremblay/Listo Films Photo, used with permission

Nakuset is Cree from Lac La Ronge, Sask. Adopted as part of the 60's scoop, she uses the experience to improve the lives of urban Aboriginal people in Montreal.

Trace L. Hentz

2

Sakathén:ti

Joy Meness (Iroquois)

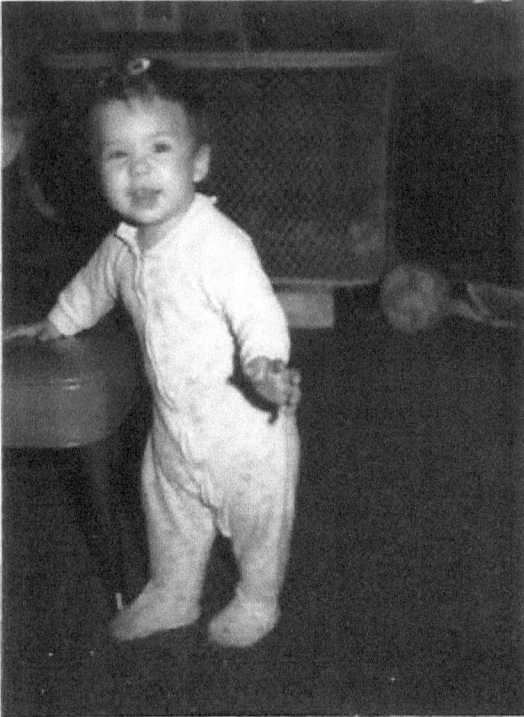

Joy Meness 9 mos.

Historical Background

Forced assimilation for the Indigenous people of who found themselves on what was now the southern side of the border between the United States and Canada, had begun with the Indian Removal Act of 1830 which had forcibly cleared much of the east coast of its Indian population. Residential boarding schools such as Carlisle Indian Industrial School (1879-1918) had then begun the next phase of the colonization process through legally mandated education.

By taking Indian children away from their families, the schools had stripped them of their language and culture. While complete absorption into American society had been thought to be possible through education, the US government realized that far too many generations of Indians were still retaining their Native ways, and their identities (McDade, 2008). So as the residential boarding school era for Indian children drew to a protracted close in the 1950s, the foster care system began to experience unprecedented growth, when children who would have otherwise been sent to boarding schools now became wards of the state.

Since the removal period the United States has implemented federal policies resulting in tribal relocation, termination, and at times imprisonment as a means to isolate Indians from society, and each other. These policies provided some support for assimilationist efforts, however by segregating children away from their families the effects of the residential boarding schools and foster care system were unintentionally aiding in the births of Native babies outside of what many might consider to be 'Christian wedlock.' In reality babies were being born away from what could have been supportive home communities due to parental displacement. The causes for these seemingly unplanned pregnancies were vast, in some cases the residential school boarding students had been molested and raped by those entrusted to care for them, in others foster parents and guardians were similarly guilty of abusing the young people in their care. (Truth and Reconciliation Commission, 2015).

Ultimately, the young people who had been raised away from their communities in institutionalized settings possessed a limited understanding, if any at all, of how babies were created and/or cared for (Harness, 2008). Although nature won out over nurture and new generations of children were still being born despite the government's best efforts to sterilize Native women. However, their parents and grandparents were at times powerless to stop their removal to the boarding schools, foster care system, and ultimately the adoption industry. What removal, relocation, and residential schools couldn't destroy, it was hoped that the government's Indian Adoption Project (1958-1967) could and would with total assimilation (Fanshel, 1972). This project, conceived from statistical calculations and an ignorance of how Native communities were interconnected, was doomed to fail from the start.

First proposed as a model, the Indian Adoption Project (IAP) was created to place 50-100 "unwanted" Indian children, who had been in foster care and residential schools, into white homes. It was hoped that this would stimulate the adoptions of Indian children as an alternative to the schools and foster care. Later the IAP would be modified to include the widespread sale of Native infants.[1] By selling the children it was hoped that the Native children could still be removed from their homes, and instead of costing the government money to assimilate them, this would be a way to make a program of removal economically self-sustaining. While selling children was not a new idea, with official institutional backing it became a well-organized industry and implemented across North America (Balcom, 2011, Fanshel, 1972, p.35). Between the IAP and the Latter Day Saints' Indian Placement Program, it is estimated that over 100,000 Indian children were removed from their families and placed for adoption with white people between 1947 and 2000. The government had cast a wide net and no Native child was safe.

While the Indian Child Welfare Act (1978) was designed and enacted to prohibit these kinds of adoptions, the onslaught of children removed by local and state governments to foster care increased as a way to skirt ICWA guidelines. Yet illegal placements continue with the sale and forced adoption of children like Veronica Brown.[2] According to the National Council of Juvenile and Family Court Judges, the Indigenous of the Americas lose custody of their children to at a higher rate than any other group of people (Sullivan, 2011). Generations of Native children and adults have become the foundation of the welfare state in America, as the United States and Canadian governments repeatedly condemn a sovereign way of life for anyone other than it's own citizens. The unspoken message here is clear, Native Americans were, and are, being deemed as unfit to raise their own children or to act on their own behalf.

Combine that double standard with Christianity and the moral ideology that accompanies it, and you have an American society that has sought to eradicate Indigenous identities in any way possible. [3] Not only were Indians coerced into becoming Christians, they were left with little alternative in refusing, to do so often meant death. One of the more insidious methods of colonization was the promotion of European standards of beauty, methods that called for the physical altering of Indigenous appearances. This meant that for generations Native people have been forced to hide in plain site in order to physically assimilate into mainstream American society. This altering of appearances began with the residential schools as all children had their hair cut and restyled upon arrival. Many were too young to realize that these changes would become habits of a lifetime, instilled in them through an education beyond their control. At the Carlisle Indian Industrial School not only did they cut student's hair, photographs were taken of them as well and then altered so that their skin would appear lighter.[4]

Taking on the appearance of the institution is common and also occurs in the military. Those who join often do so by choice and by cutting their hair and wearing a uniform military personnel are seen as being representative of their government. Residential schools were frequently not a choice for children, rather education was imposed upon them, and today when former students are viewed only through the lens of the residential schools it does them a disservice. It forever associates them with a time in their life that many may not want to recall or have chosen.

What's worse is that many of these appearance-altering practices are still going on when Native people are incarcerated. One of the first things that happens when a Native person goes to jail is that their hair is cut, and of course they then have to wear prison issue clothing, which is exactly what happened to the children at the residential schools.

So where once Native people were forced to wear the uniforms of the institutions they were being assimilated by, they now have adapted to American society and wear blue jeans and business suits by choice. Today most Native people dress in the clothing and style of their oppressors without realizing the models of beauty they are perpetuating. The message was clear, conform to societies' standards of body image and beauty—or face the consequences.

If removing Native languages and altering peoples' outer appearances weren't enough, further attempts were made to change the way Indians thought, in the hopes that by eradicating traditional belief systems through forced Christianization, that Indians would wholly be absorbed into American society. These widespread efforts to replace traditional ways with Judeo-Christian beliefs caused cognitive dissonance and cultural fractures within Native communities. Today, intergenerational trauma is frequently found in Indian Country as 500 years of colonization takes its toll.

By forcing people to convert to Christianity and speak English in order to survive, a different way of thinking has manifested in Native communities. Beliefs have changed in response to the English only education, and not for the better. Alcoholism, drug use, domestic violence, child abuse, sexual abuse, rape, PTSD, missing women and men, high (and often unjust) rates of incarceration for both men and women, suicide, diabetes, cancer, and thyroid disorders are just a few of the many issues that American Indians deal with today. There is not one Native family who hasn't experienced the residential schools in some fashion or been affected by these issues. It didn't used to be this way.

My Place in History

Yet this is a common story, it could be about every person on the planet who has ever had to endure forced assimilation. It is a story about what Indigenous people have suffered for centuries in their own homeland, no matter the situation experiences and traumas are the same. It is my story.

Dedication

The writing of this chapter is in memory of my good friend Mike Martel, *Ojibwe*, who left us too soon—but not before he taught me that no matter what I had suffered during my exile/adoption I was never alone or far from home. I was adopted, Mike had been a prisoner of the foster care system. He survived because the dogs he had been chained up with shared their food with him. He used to say, "they couldn't beat the Indian out of me, they only drove it deeper" and then he would laugh. No truer words could have been spoken for us all. The call of our ancestors, which has been encoded in our DNA, remains strong. Assimilation hasn't won as our hearts lead us and guide us home.

An Overview of My Beginning: The Story and the Myth

As a child I knew that I was adopted, but that was all. My name, my parents, even my ethnicity would remain shrouded in mystery until I was old enough to look for my parents. There was nothing transparent about my adoption either; I had no information about who I was before I was taken away from my mother. Even today my adoption papers have been kept from me.

But when I was young and I asked who I was, I was told the usual lies; that my parents were too young to take care of me, that they wanted me to have a better life, that they didn't have money to raise me, etc. Then and now those answers made no sense, nor were they true. As any adopted person on the planet can tell you, there must be a handbook given to people with these kinds of blanket answers that explains why they're raising someone elses child and not their own.

But my adoption information was not to be shared in public, my origins were a mystery, and as I got older I could only imagine what was so wrong with me that my identity had to have been kept such a closely guarded secret. Yet, time and time again I would be reminded of my status as an adopted person in a million little ways, just never in public. Appearances must be maintained. The comments, the inherent racism, it was all there. It was made very clear to me early on that I wasn't wanted by anyone, not my real family and certainly not by these people who had adopted me. So despite their wish that my origins remain a secret, (I was a truth teller even back then) I shared my information whenever the opportunity presented itself. And so, by the time I was an adult they would not speak of my adoption at all, changing the subject every time I mentioned it.

1967

So after years of sorting and sifting information, the following is the best version of events that I can reconstruct. I appear to have been born in the fall of 1967, on the 20th of November, although of the date I am not certain.[5] I was born during a time in American history when Indians were thought of as less than dogs in many places. There were signs in the south and the west, which read, "No Dogs, No Indians Allowed." Today if you look hard enough you can find that some of those signs are still there. I was told many, many times in my life that I was lucky to be considered as Caucasian. I disagree.

This was also the era of Civil Rights, and although legally segregation was becoming a thing of the past, in 1967 not much had changed in terms of the way white people and the government treated Native people. Since that time things have gotten better for Native people in some ways, and in others—they've become worse. These were the times I was born into and I realize being Native was not thought of as a good thing in American society at that time. A lot of people over the years have told me that I was better off by being adopted out, but the price I paid for the life I now have? It was high.

So despite the fact that I am highly educated, I have to be careful that I don't contribute to the ongoing processes of assimilation. European ways are not traditional Native ways, they never were. Since the United States is a capitalistic country where money drives not only the economy, but is the underpinning of every aspect of society, including adoption, it is easy to forget that it is also the reason why things were the way they were at that time.

The Costs of Adoption

News stories today talk about the high cost of adoption, especially for white babies, and it makes me wonder if as a person of colour I was somehow less expensive, maybe worth less than a white child.[6] Certainly that's the message that's been played out in the media, that people of colour are worth less than their white counterparts, if this weren't true then there wouldn't be groups such as Black Lives Matter.

The whole process of placing children in homes other than their own has a financial component, and personally, I equate the adoption process with money changing hands. It's that way no matter if a child is in foster care, education, or adoption; there are dollar signs on the head of every person in America, and a child is worth more.[7] I have a receipt from the adoption agency stating that the people who bought me paid $500. Today adoption costs can run into the tens of thousands of dollars, who is benefiting from these costs? The agencies, lawyers, and the state. I certainly never benefited from it.

The Fairy Tale

During the 1950s and 60s children were an essential part of the American Dream, most women were expected to stay at home, taking care of their families and being good housewives. Those who couldn't have their own children, and were willing to pay a price to satisfy the societal demand for the perfect family, bought their children from whatever source they could find, legal or not. Since the people who adopted me had both worked at two children's homes: the Methodist Home for Children in Mechanicsburg, Pennsylvania, and the Upstate Baptist Children's Home in Oneonta, New York; in the eyes of society they were more than qualified to raise me instead of my own family.

My adoption took place during the 1960s on the heels of the Jim Crow era, a time when people of colour were treated like second-class citizens, and oh how I was. The people who adopted me were white, Republican, religious, middle class people who wanted a child, and since girls were thought to adapt more easily to adoption, I didn't stand a chance. It was as if a fairy tale had been written about me and I was cast as the unwitting main character.[8] My adoption was meant to transform their life into some sort of utopia. However their acceptance into white society was absolute; my presence would only be tolerated. I spent a lot of my childhood wondering what I'd done to make people so angry. But then that was the same kind of hypocritical thinking that had precipitated the ease with which my adoption went through. These people had wanted a child at all costs, and nothing else mattered. Never mind that I would be an Indian in a White world, no one ever considered what that would mean to me.

The Gaps Between Fact and Fiction

They told me that they had gotten me in November of 1967, supposedly just days after I was born. Some versions of the story had me coming to them when I was 6 days old, others at 9 days. After I had my own children I realized that I could recite without thinking my kid's birthdays, what time they had been born, and how much they had weighed, I wondered why my story varied so much. Shouldn't it have been a significant time for them, the details important enough to remember? They said they had known they were getting me and had spent months preparing for my arrival, how then could they not know on what day I arrived? Clearly it was not in November of 1967.

At that time the woman who adopted me had her parents living with her, and although her father died in March of 1968, her mother, a first generation German immigrant, continued to stay with her and her husband. So growing up I heard three different versions of the circumstances surrounding my adoption, and not one account matched the other. Besides not knowing what day I arrived on, I was told that my arrival had been a surprise. This certainly didn't mesh with the other version that had them planning for me.

The Evidence

Since the camera was invented people have been finding new ways to collect, store, and display images. It was no different in the house where I grew up. There was a collection of picture albums beginning in the 1950s which were regularly added to each year. If they'd gotten me in November of '67 where were my baby pictures? There were pictures of a baby shower that was supposed to be for me, but if I was a surprise why wasn't I in them? I was always told I was at that shower, so why didn't the photographs demonstrate that?

However, in 1962 these people had tried to adopt a little boy and it hadn't worked out, after eight months he went back to his family. I think the pictures I was shown were from the baby shower they'd had when they tried to adopt that little boy. Growing up the furniture in my room had been blue. The truth was that there had been no preparation for me, only for that little boy. I had been a surprise, and not just in my arrival. Later there would be clues as to my past, although it would take until I was an adult for me to realize them.

So the first photograph album I appeared in showed me sitting in a high chair. There were also pictures of me walking. As an adult I knew when milestones occurred, if those were pictures of me then they were taken in 1968—or later. There was not one image of me needing to be held and supported as a newborn. These were stunning realizations that would occupy my mind and raise further questions, which drove my determination to find out the truth.

Still, there were no baby pictures of me during the early part of 1968. I began to wonder where was I? Where had I been? Surely I'd been somewhere since no infant takes care of itself. There were too many little things wrong with the stories I'd been told to ignore the inconsistencies the evidence provided. Later I would find out that I was most likely still with my mother during that time, although the possibility does exist that I had been in foster care as. With no records it's hard to know just where I was.

Yet despite the time gap, according to my amended birth certificate, my adoption was finalized in August of 1968, effectively sealing my identity and my fate for many years to come. Mine was a closed adoption, as most in New York State are, and my records remain sealed still.

By 1969 they'd moved and I grew up six miles away from the nearest Iroquois Indians on the Tuscarora Reservation near Sanborn, NY. Being that close to a reservation as a child would later come to play a large role in my life, although at the time I was unaware of its significance.

Doubts

The questions remain, why did they move to Lewiston so quickly after my adoption? They bought their house in the winter, no one in New York State buys a house then, you can't see a house properly with all that snow. Why did he give up his job at the church to work full time at the hospital in Niagara Falls? Never again would he be the minister at a church. I stayed at the Lewiston house with them until the wife died of cancer in March of 1977. Eventually her mother moved out when he remarried, and I remained there with him and his second wife. I would fare no better with his second wife, she resented my presence and during my high school years I would begin to realize how alone I really was.

The Absurdity of It All

In the end I realize that I was an unrealistic expectation in making someone else's dream a reality. By the time I was in high school the people I stayed with no more wanted me than I wanted them, and when we all figured that out it was far too late to do anything about it. I'm sure they must have thought they'd adopted a dud. I had all the chance of pleasing them as an apple seed does of growing into an orange tree.

In some respects I was taken care of, but the people I lived with during my childhood and teenage years were all incredibly abusive, each in their own way. The arguing and violence that took place behind closed doors was always denied in public for the sake of "what will people think?" After the first wife died and that man remarried all his religious ideals sailed out the window, never to be seen again. He'd gone from pretending in public that he never smoked or drank to doing both on a daily basis in his home. He and his second wife drank wine or beer before dinner, with dinner, and after dinner they often switched to hard liquor. They were in their late 40s then, and how they ever made it to work each day is beyond me. Yet the pretense of superiority was always present. They were Christians, and as such they believed they deserved to be thought of as on a moral pedestal.

Of course I realize now that the events I am recalling didn't happen overnight, that kind of tolerance to alcohol takes years to cultivate. Nor did the hypocrisy, it was a way of life and I was a constant threat that their secret way of life would be revealed. It was dysfunctualism at it's finest. These would be dark times of isolation for me, a solitary confinement of the middle class, separated by the boundaries between race and class. It was all I knew and I had nowhere and no one, to turn to. I had been taken prisoner in a 500-year cultural war of colonization, complete with psychological warfare. I had been assimilated and held against my will, beaten when I would not comply with their demands.

The foundation for all of this was of course religion. Theirs. They were as absolute in their beliefs and I was in mine. I recognized that their religion was nothing more than a pretense and an excuse by which to hurt me. I had learned from them that when people said one thing they meant and did another, and that combined with my adopter's outright lies made it impossible for me to trust anyone. When I think about my childhood I remember a child who was often sick, constantly drugged with 'medicines' and unbelievably confused as to how the world worked. What I knew inside did not match the world around me, it was a vast area of spiritual wasteland. Desolate, I didn't how to survive the situation I found myself in.

Whose Truth?

As a child to me the word adopted meant different so my equating my adoption with being unlike the people I knew would be understandable after finding out I was an American Indian. Yet I didn't grow up with that knowledge, and if I had known what would it have meant?

I had been allowed to identify with white culture and even though I had done my best to emulate the society which surrounded me, I knew that I was never going to be like anyone else. After graduating from high school I was finally, after years of pleading, taken to the adoption agency for my information. It was then that I was told I was a Native American. And the sad truth was that I didn't know what that meant. All I knew about Indians at that moment was that they were savages who scalped people.[9]

Yet other people knew who I was, I thought of several incidents that now made sense. The time my 9th grade social studies teacher pointed out to the whole class how dark I was in comparison to the other students. When I went to summer school and on the way home through the reservation and my adopter pulled over in front of a house that looked as though no one had lived there in quite a long time and shouted, "Do you want to live like these people? Do you?"

I did.

Anything would be better than the life I knew, but fear ruled my life and I couldn't function. I had identified with my captors and had hated every moment of my time with them, their belief system, and their way of life. It took me a long time as an adult to leave those things, and those people behind. It would take until I returned to college in my thirties before my story actually became about me. Up until then I only existed in relation to everyone I had known. I had no idea who I was.

But I knew there was something wrong with me. In social gatherings when people would tell stories the only ones I knew (if I even dared to share them) were always met with silence, never laughter. In time I realized that I had never known happiness, only survival. My life had been in response to the circumstances that had surrounded me. Returning to college was the best thing that could have happened to me, it was a new beginning for my kids and I. During this time I decided to resume my search for my parents.

ICWA & Finding My Way Home

Fittingly I began searching again by contacting the adoption agency that was supposed to have handled my adoption, the Lutheran Services Society, of Buffalo NY. As I don't fall under the parameters of the Indian Child Welfare Act (ICWA) of 1978, there was little I could do to open my records, and of course the adoption agency wouldn't give me identifying information. But at that time in New York State, for a fee, an adoptee could get a copy their actual records with the identifying information blacked out. But I had made the mistake of believing my adopter when he said that he wanted to help, and when I told him what I was doing and he called the adoption agency and blocked my records. I received a call from the man who worked at the adoption agency saying that he was sorry he couldn't help me, and then I received a form letter in the mail containing nothing of any relevance. Once again my records were being kept from me, I took it as a sign that I was on the right track.

Never again would I tell my adopter what I was doing, it felt like I was always falling into the same old traps, and giving people chances to help me build a new life weren't working. I was starting to recognize this disappointment as a constant theme in my life. At that time in my life everyone close to me had wanted to stop me from living my own life, wanting me to be the same person they had tried to force me to be, compliant and dependent upon them for every little thing. Education had emboldened me; it wasn't going to be so easy to control me anymore.

It was at this point that I realized there was something wrong with my adoption if people were working so hard to stop me from finding out the truth. I started to think my adoption had been illegal, maybe there were no records. I would have to find out who I was a different way.

I continued going to college, but as a single parent who worked and went to college, finding my own parents during that time wasn't exactly a priority. So even though I knew at that point I was an Indian—and that information was informing my learning, beyond that I didn't know what to do next. Going to the nearest reservation and knocking on doors didn't seem like such a good idea. So instead I did what I had always done, I read. Books had been my refuge as a child, my escape as an adult, and so now I read everything that I could find about Indians. It was an education like none other. I was able to connect with a past that had been denied to me through the voices of authors that now came through time and space to speak to me.

Reconfiguring My Inner & Outer Space

They say there is no sound in outer space, that the human ear can detect nothing. There is darkness, a void so large that it is a billion light years across. Outer space has no breathable air, and without an air tank, a human being suffocates.

This is the place that I existed when I was adopted. I had lost everything. My parents, my culture, my language, and my identity. I did not exist.

They also say that a human being in a sensory deprivation chamber can hear their blood pulse. A heartbeat is like a drum beat, and yet slowed down time stops, the universe stands still.

I know that place too. It's the place where light can exist.

So in the darkest hour on earth as the planet turns toward the sun, the spark of life in the blood in my veins leads me home. *O'tónhkwa*

There was never just one moment which defined my homecoming. It wasn't like what you see on Oprah, there was no emotional reunion being filmed, and there certainly wasn't a huge party. Instead it was more like a thousand little moments where I had choices to make as to which direction I wanted my life to go in. I know who I am now, and I can trace my life backwards, understanding how if it weren't for the residential boarding schools, I would never have been caught up into the adoption industry. But if it weren't for the education that I have I wouldn't be where I am now. So in some respects the process that was designed to destroy American Indians has saved me, and in that everything can become a circle and become complete.[10]

Education

When I was born in 1967 Indians were often thought of as not good enough for many things, such as being a lawyer or a doctor. Even though Americanized education has been mandated for all Native children for over a century, few are ever allowed to graduate high school—let alone achieve degrees in higher education. It's a system designed to not only to withhold information, but marginalize anyone who doesn't conform to the process. Of course this has attracted non-conformists like me to education for that very reason. I found university to be the place where I was accepted, and that there were people there who truly wanted to help others. Of course there were a few there that weren't quite so helpful, but again, if you take those moments as learning experiences then it's possible to come full circle and move on in life.

I am one of the fortunate adoptees, I was able to go home, learn my language—and get my education. Therefore my hope in sharing this story is that there will come a time when no longer will we as Indigenous people have to endure what generations of residential boarding school students, foster care children, and adoptees did. Many lost everything, their names, their culture, and some their lives.

Today we are still in a 500-year war against colonization, a system that seeks to continuously establish the mandates of the Doctrine of Discovery. Through genocidal practices, as defined by the United Nations in 1948, the murder, enslavement, sterilization, and transference of Native children to other people, has threatened to destroy us as a people for centuries. By telling stories like mine we uncover a history that has been hidden away through revisionism. It then becomes possible to make education work for us and not against us.

Everything always comes full circle, birth, death, the seasons, our lives, the cycle always continues. If you leave something undone you always get another chance to finish it. So I believe that we all have the chance to go home, and that possibility is always there. Every opportunity, every interaction with another family member means that I am always going home, and that never ends. However, the government still won't release my records, so that remains unfinished for me.

Wa'konnonwveráhton táhnon wake'nikonrí:yo
~ Being Grateful and having a Good Mind

The *Ohén:ton Karihwehtékwen* or the words before all else, which many people call the Thanksgiving Address, is used as an opening at many Roti'nonshón:ni gatherings. The words that come before all else speak to us as human beings of our place in the circle, and how we are all related to the earth, the universe, and each other. The Thanksgiving Address teaches us how to be grateful for the circle of life and how to bring our minds together as one. It is recited before a gathering, and then used again as a closing. If it is not used again as a closing, then the circle is left open.

I believe that is what has happened to us with our adoptions, the circle was left open and it is up to each and every one of us to learn the words, and our truth, in order for those circles to be closed. So for now my circle remains open, as does many others. I believe that by bringing our minds together as one and sharing our stories, many circles will close, not just our own. So as I send this story out into the Universe—may you find what you are looking for, here, within these words.

REFERENCES

Balcom, K. (2011). The Traffic in Babies: Cross-Border Adoption and Baby-Selling between the United States and Canada, 1930-1972

Devan Harness, S. (2008). *Mixing Cultural Identities Through Transracial Adoption: Outcomes of the Indian Adoption Project (1958-1967).* Lewiston: The Edwin Mellen Press.

Fanshel, D. (1972). *Far From the Reservation: The Transracial Adoption of American Indian Children.* New Jersey: The Scarecrow Press, Inc.

McDade, J. (2008). *The Birth of the American Indian Manual Labor Boarding School.* Lewiston: The Edwin Mellen Press.

Sullivan, L. (2011). *Native Foster Care*, All Things Considered, National Public Radio.

Truth and Reconciliation Commission of Canada Final Report, (2015). Montreal: McGill-Queen's University Press.

FOOTNOTES

[1] The government's definition of an unwanted child presumed a nuclear family structure and excluded extended family members, including but not limited to a child's grandparents, aunts or uncles, and often older cousins. If for any reason the mother or father of a child was not present in their life then this was grounds for removal.

[2] Veronica Brown's father was not notified of her impending adop-

tion under ICWA regulations and she was returned to him for two years. In a stunning reversal two years later, Baby Veronica was given to them by the Supreme Court.

[3] One of the best examples of this is the Anglicized picture of Jesus which portrays him as fair with light coloured eyes despite him being of Middle Eastern descent.

[4] See the work of John Nicholas Choate in association with the Carlisle Indian School.

[5] Many adoptees, although it seems to be mostly Indians, ages were changed to discourage the uncovering of records and illegal adoptions.

[6] Not only are adoptions expensive, millions of dollars have been spent on the incarceration, education, and foster care systems built on the backs of Native people.

[7] See the high cost of incarcerating prisoners in America.

[8] There are times when my life has felt like the main character in The Truman Show did, life was all a lie and everyone knew the true story but me.

[9] This the recollection that caused me to understand why I became an educator.

[10] The motto of the Carlisle Indian Industrial School was, "Kill the Indian, and Save the Man". General Richard H. Pratt.

3

Enrolled

Belinda Mastalski Smith (Oneida New York)

I was adopted at birth by two great folks, Andrew and Angela Mastalski. For 40 years they were the only parents I knew. The letter my parents received from the adoption agency said my birth mother was from a Northeastern tribe and my father was a small part Cherokee. I found out later that I also had six sisters and brothers.

Soon after I was born I had open heart surgery. While my parents had a chance to return me to the agency, they chose to keep me. My Dad likes to tell people they had to, they had lost the receipt! At the age of 37 I started having chest pains. My Dad insisted I look for my family so I could find out my medical history.

After lots of nagging, I finally registered with a site I found online. I thought nothing more about it. Three years later, out of the blue, I got an email from a woman who thought she was my birth cousin. What a shock! I slammed the lid of my laptop and told no-one, not even my husband, about the message. I received another message about a week later saying that the woman realized this was a shock, and that the family really just wanted to be sure I was OK. If I wanted no contact after that it was OK with them.

We communicated back and forth and exchanged photos. I was sent an early photo of a boy and girl who would be my full blood brother and sister if this woman's theory was true. When I saw the photo of the boy, something just told me we were related.

The state of Massachusetts had just passed a law that anyone who was adopted and was now over the age of 18, could request a copy of their original birth certificate. I got this search under way. This was October, the new law did not go into effect until January 1, so we had a wait. In the meantime I was able to request further information regarding my adoption from the state office through which it was coordinated. It was a long wait for this information as well, but on New Year's Eve 2007, I received a letter regarding my file. It listed the names of my brothers and sisters. I immediately called the woman who thought she was my cousin, and told her the names. It was true! I was her cousin and I had located my birth family, or we had located each other. We cried and cried.

Nine years later the excitement and tears are still there as I tell this story. Within days my cousin Kandice would contact all my siblings and my birth father and let them know I had been located. Within three weeks I would be in upstate New York meeting everyone and enrolling in the Oneida Indian Nation.

It has been a whirlwind since then. Many visits with my family. Sometimes as many as seven visits a year. My birth mother passed away three years before I was found. I also had a brother pass away soon after birth. The Nation has provided me with funding for my Master of Public Administration, which I earned in 2011, as well as my Master of Arts in History, that I am working on right now. I hope to use this degree to eventually work in a Native American Museum or teach Native American History. My ultimate goal is to one day work for my Nation and give back to them in appreciation for what they have provided for me.

I have included a photo of me with three of my sisters, my brother and my birth dad as we put a wreath on my birth-mothers grave when I was in NY last week.

December 2015, far right, Belinda Mastalski Smith (Oneida New York)

4

Unceded Children of Disconnect

Rebecca Larsen (Quinault Indian Nation)

I'd like to take a moment to introduce myself. My name is Rebecca Larsen. I am a proud member of the Quinault Indian Nation of western Washington. My mother was born Karen Myrtle Black of the Black family of the Quileute Nation. My grandmother was Myrtle Black, who was ¾ Quileute ¼ Hoh; my great-grandmother was Violet Black (Bright), who was ½ Quileute ½ Hoh, when she married my great-grandfather Carl James Black Sr., Ka-la-dwok, full blooded Quileute, and my great-great grandparents were James Black, full blooded Quileute, born in 1854, and Jennie Black, full blooded Quileute, born in 1852.

I take the time to introduce myself in this manner as is the custom of our people to delineate the line of ancestors from which we come.

I say it proudly and with a strong voice that these Ancestors stand behind me and with me, as I have made this journey. I know today that they walked the other world when looking for me and for my mother, the Unceded Children who were stolen from them, and how they looked for me as diligently as I have searched for them.

Many aspects of my life today are a direct result of an active Bureau of Indian Affairs agent who oversaw the Southwest region of Washington. My story begins with my grandmother Myrtle Black who from what facts I've been able to gather was ill for some reason or possibly in the hospital for childbirth during the Scoop Era years. My mother was two or three years old at that time (long before the Indian Child Welfare Act came into place to protect our tribal children.)

Becky in foster care

There was a time for us as Indian people when the Bureau of Indian affairs secretly funded, sanctioned and cooperated with the Indian Adoption Projects and funded the Child Welfare League in the

United States. This was the era after the boarding schools had proven to be an absolute failure at forced assimilation of our people and our children. This period was commonly known as "the Scoop" in the United States and in Canada. It became common practice to literally "scoop" as many of our children off our reservations as possible, to literally snatch our Native children from their homes, yards, or schools and move them quickly into the Child Welfare League or the Indian Adoption Projects warehouses.

My mother remembered the day that she was taken from her home along with two of her siblings and loaded into a car and taken away. She was a terrified little girl and was given no explanation as to where she was being taken or why—she just remembered crying as her brother was taken into a separate car. She was never to see her mother, my grandmother again… let that sink in a moment.

She was taken that day into custody by the State of Washington and placed very quickly for adoption in Oregon. This was the practice at the time: to remove Indian children swiftly and take them far away from their families and from their tribal communities, giving their communities and families no recourse to find them. They didn't even know where to begin. The Indian agent superintendent would stonewall them long enough for adoptions to be "finalized" and then they would be told, "Oh, I am sorry, you did not act quickly enough. They have already been adopted by a family in another state and their records have been sealed for their protection."

My mother remembers that day as it was the day that scarred her for the rest of her life. She was adopted very quickly into a family in Oregon whereupon her birth certificate was altered to show that these strangers had given "birth" to her and were her parents. The BIA fully funded this so-called scoop of our children and moved quickly to pass legislation to seal permanently the case files of these children so that no link could be tied to them. Once birth certificates were altered, there was no going back.

There were often books of photographs created by a the Indian Adoption Projects of photographs of Native children of varying ages who were living in orphanages or temporary boarding houses created specifically as clearinghouses and for the trafficking of our children. Prospective adoptive parents looked at these "books," these pictures and pointed at a picture of an Indian child they wanted to choose and that's how the decision was made as to who they would adopt. This is how my mother was adopted into her family in Oregon.

The family that adopted my mother, Karen, were not good people. She was abused physically and emotionally by people who were supposed to take care of her and to love her. She had a feeling of disconnection with them and never really felt part of this family. She knew in her young heart that she had been stolen from her mother, and her family. Fast forward 13 years and she finds herself pregnant with me as a teenager. This family makes a quick decision to send her away to an unwed mother's boarding school; they still had them in those days. This place was yet another clearinghouse, another brokerage house for our children… another guarantee of more children being further disconnected from our culture and our communities. And let's face it; little babies are a hot commodity no matter what the color.

While she was there she was further abused and assaulted by staff and by the nuns who are supposed to protect her and to help her during her pregnancy with me. When the time came that April and she went into labor with me, she was forced against her will and against her wishes, to sign "voluntary" relinquishment and closed adoption papers for me. She was not given a choice in this matter… and she was scared and alone and had already been coerced with beatings and rape. She was never allowed to see me or to hold me. When I was taken from her she ran away from that place never to return home to the people who adopted her.

With little education and no money and no connections, she turned to the streets of Seattle and Portland, where many of our displaced tribal people gathered in some concentration. (Another failed project of the Urban Relocation Projects, but that is another story). She immediately felt connected to these Indian people, but there her drinking began in earnest to numb the feelings that she had. Not only did she know that she been stolen from her mother, her people and her tribal community but to numb the feeling of knowing that I had been stolen from her. She lived for many years in this life on the streets. But I was not to know this for many years.

Now, I too am a child placed in the system, a commodity to be used by the State but now of Oregon, not even the State of my People. I am placed in a foster home in Bend where I lived blissfully with a wonderful family who cared for me and loved me for the first three years of my life. And all was well during this time and then one day (according to my foster parents) my caseworker found out that I attended church with them every Sunday at the same small church that my mother's adoptive family also attended. Of course, this case worker did not know that my mother Karen was now living on the streets in Portland or that my mother, just as her mother, my grandmother, was unaware that I am alive and living in the same small town where she had once lived.

Now, come back to the secrecy surrounding the adoption of us as Indian people... its success is all built on secrets and lies and cover up. My caseworker immediately panicked, (again according to my foster parents) that my grandparents or my mother might recognize me in church. The genes in my family are SO strong... I look SO much like my mother, my daughter looks SO much like me, it is unmistakable to make familial connection.

With almost no time given to my foster parents who raised me since birth, the State told them to prepare to send me to an adoptive home. This family did everything in their power to keep me. They petitioned to adopt me themselves and were denied, they were simply told that the caseworker felt that they were not young enough to raise a child of my age. They would have been in their fifties at the time this was happening. This was the reason they were given as to why they were being denied. So, at that point their adult daughter who was also married, petitioned to adopt me, to keep me within this family. She and her husband were also denied. This all happened very quickly, within a week my caseworker had found a family that was willing to adopt an older Native American child. They too were shown a book with my picture in it along with other Native children, another adoption clearinghouse of our Indian children. They picked me out of this book and consented to adopt me.

I remember the day that I met them with my caseworker in a city park in Bend and we fed the swans …I remember what I was wearing that day… a red and white checkered dress with black dress shoes and a red woolen coat… I remember meeting these strangers and being told that very soon they would be my parents. Within a very short period of time my things were packed. I stood outside the only home I had ever known and I was handed over to these people. My records at that time also became sealed along with my fate and my birth certificate was altered to show these strangers had given birth to me.

The one good thing that my new adopted mother was able to do during this process when left alone by the caseworker who had my files spread out on her desk, was to lean over to look at the names that were noted on the papers that were open in my file. She quickly wrote down the names which were very unique and put them away in her purse. One name, I was to find out later was the name of my mother's adoptive family. And the second name was the very unique name of my foster parents—this she also tucked away in her purse. Without these two names and even without her quick thinking, I would not be writing this story today, so I owe her that.

At this point I was four years old when I was loaded into their car and taken away; I remember that day. I remember the feeling disconnect, the overwhelming sense of loss and confusion about where I was going. Who were these people that I did not know, these complete strangers? Why were they calling themselves my parents. I desperately wanted to be back with my "family."

As it turned out, my adopted mother was ill-equipped to be a parent and really shouldn't have been allowed to be one but now she was mine. So for the next eight or nine years, I lived with this family carrying their name. Where I too, just like my mother, was abused and mistreated and molested by the people who were supposed to love me and take care of me.

We moved often. I have come to realize we did so because my adopted father didn't want to be found out by neighbors or community members because he was also mistreating my mother and if my mother made friends or became close to people in the community—or if I did, it was a sure indication that we would take flight, pack in the middle of the night, and move to another small town. So I learned not to make friends… for like my family, they would be taken from me. It was a lonely, frightening life of disconnection.

As a young pre-teen this turned into a blessing in disguise for me. For at this point, by my last recollection, I had gone to 18 different schools, although some of them were repeats, as we would move up and down the Oregon/Washington coast and sometimes lived in the same place twice. The blessing came when we moved back to La Connor, Washington, which is the home to the Swinomish tribal community.

I remember that dread of walking into school in the sixth grade and two Indian boys in the back of the class yelled out my name Becky Brown! I remember thinking, how odd that these two boys who I had been friends with in the second grade still lived in the same community and still went to the same school... it was such a strange concept to me. I thought that my strange life was the normal one. But I remember my Indian being so grateful to see them... (If you are Indigenous you know this feeling in your soul).

I settled almost immediately into a wonderful space in this small tribal community. There is something about us as Indian people... something inside of us that speaks so loudly, so loudly to our spirit of who we are, of how we long to be together in community no matter where we have been raised. Our Indian knows...I have come to believe today that my ancestors knew that this was where I needed to be and they settled that day, the day I came back here. These are not my People but they have become my family and I would not be here today without them or this community.

I began "working" for a Tribal youth program. I think it was really just a volunteer program that summer, mostly to keep us out of trouble but the Youth Director at that time took us on. My two young friends and I were put to work on a basketball court for the youth, when some small voice in my heart told me to tell this man what was going on in my adoptive home. At this point in my young life, I had already begun to contemplate suicide. If things did not change, I had already begun to think that it was a viable option to the miserable existence I was living.

So I told him, and that wonderful man didn't hesitate for a moment. He said you're leaving that place and you're moving in with me and my family. I went home that day and I packed my few belongings and never went back. My adoptive father came one time to their house to try to retrieve me. They met him at the door; they told him that he was on Indian land that I was a Native girl and I would never be going home with them again. And if they tried to force me against my will, he would call tribal police and have him arrested. My parents never came again and I never saw my adopted father the rest of my life.

Of course, they needed a story to tell the rest of my adoptive family where I was, for suddenly one day I was just gone and no longer part of the family. I had grown half siblings, my adoptive father's children, and many nieces and nephews, so they had to tell people something. They concocted the story that I'd been a problem for them the whole time they had me, that I was just some Indian girl anyway, that it didn't matter where I was or that I didn't live with them anymore. And that I was telling lies to people about them as my parents and how ungrateful I was.

And of course the rest of my adoptive family believed them. Which is **exactly** the story my mother's adopted family spewed to me when I met them, how ungrateful my mother was, how she had told terrible lies about them, how she should have been thankful that they gave her a home when her mother threw her away? I have met countless other Native adoptees who were told exactly the same thing—why aren't we just grateful to our great white savior parents?

Now fast-forward to me being 18 and I find myself pregnant with my beautiful daughter and I marry a high school sweetheart from my small town. I decided to take those two names my adoptive mother had written down and begin my search in the small town of my birth. As it turns out, it didn't take a lot of sleuthing. I was able to identify almost immediately my foster parents who had me in their care from birth. They were overjoyed to hear from me and couldn't wait to see me and to meet my beautiful daughter.

At this point I didn't realize what had happened to my mother by her own adoptive family—but I had their last name and within two phone calls I was able to locate them. They were also in Bend, Oregon and they seemed very happy to hear for me as well. So within two weeks I was bound for Bend on a train with my little girl to meet the people who had taken care of me and the people that I assumed were my grandparents, who I assumed had taken good care of my mother.

As fate would have it, my adopted grandparents told me that they heard very rarely from my mother, that she was living on the streets and sometimes once a year maybe twice, she would call them collect, to berate them and be angry with them on the phone, obviously drinking and then she would hang up. Occasionally, they would have an address where they could locate her to send her money or a card, but beyond that they had very little contact with her and they were honest with me about that as I made preparations to come to meet them in Oregon. But of course they did not disclose why my mother was living on the streets or why she had run away from them.

In the customs of my people, again, I believe that my ancestors interceded the day before I left Seattle on the train. My mother Karen called my adopted grandparents in Bend to be angry with them and to tell them what she thought of them and in that process, they were able to tell her that I was on my way from Seattle and that I would have a layover in Portland for four hours with my little girl.

My mother Karen told me later that she got very quiet and cried on the phone and took my number. She called me that day before I left and we made arrangements to meet in Portland during my layover before going to see her adoptive parents and my respective foster parents in Bend. I remember praying for peace and understanding that day, for understanding finally, why my mother had given me away, as this is what I still believed.

I remember taking a cab to the shelter where she lived not far from the train station, to her studio-sized room with the sink and a cot. When she opened the door, I was struck by how much I looked like her, to see my reflection mirrored back at me was the strangest feeling. I spent those four hours with Karen and she shared her story, of her broken life with me, of how things never healed in her, of how she was stolen, and then how I was I stolen from her. How she had lived a hard life on the streets, but how it was far better than the life of abuse that she had suffered at the hands of people who were supposed to love her and care for her. And during that time I shared my broken story with her… of my own life of disconnect. Healing took place that day in both of us.

I proceeded on to Bend to spend time with my wonderful foster parents. I remember walking into their house and remembering where my bedroom had been, where the stairs led to the room that I shared with another little boy whom they were allowed to adopt and who still lived with them as he was disabled. I spent a wonderful two weeks visiting with them. I shared the story of how abusive my adopted grandparents had been to my mother and although we agreed to meet them for coffee, I didn't have any further contact with them.

I went home to Seattle and renewed a relationship with my mother Karen although it was difficult at times. She lived on the streets and her drinking had increased. At times it was very hard to spend extended amounts of time or to have her in my home. This was prior to cell phones or technology—she would often disappear for long periods of time back onto the streets without any knowledge of where she'd gone or if she was still alive or safe, often jumping freight trains to California to follow the fruit picking life of a nomad. When my daughter was six or seven Karen did this again, and we did not hear from her again. My daughter and I would watch the parks in Pioneer Square or the "Indian" Park next to Pike Place Market, hoping to catch a glimpse of her or to learn that she was safe—but we had both by now conceded that she had probably passed.

Fast forward again: I believe my ancestors and hers were watching over us to bring us together. One fateful day I was on the computer talking to a friend of mine on Facebook, who happened to be the Director of the Chief Seattle Club. The Chief Seattle Club is a shelter in downtown Seattle which began as a soup kitchen and had developed into a beautiful facility which has served homeless and urban Indians for many years. It served to connect them with culture; it gave them a safe haven and provided other programs and services. I thought maybe, off chance, my mother had used their services again (since she did back in the day when it was just a soup kitchen). I asked if he would be willing to look for her name in their records and he said, give me just a moment, let me check.

Five minutes later, he came back on the computer and he said, "Call your mother, she's waiting to hear from you, here is her number." It turns out that my mother did use their services along with my half-brother, and my friend called the last contact number that my half-brother had listed on his paperwork. A woman answered the phone and he asked for my brother and the woman on the phone said, "I'm sorry he's not here. He's gone to treatment." My friend said, "Can I leave a message for him please? I know this is strange but his sister is trying to locate him and his mother." He said there was a very long pause on the phone and the woman at the other end responded, "His sister? His sister Becky is looking for us?" He said she started to cry and she said, "This is her mother."

So I was able to reconnect with my mother through a random act of technology and in two days she was able to meet her first great-grandson and spend time with her only granddaughter and me. She went with us that Easter to services and was so proud to witness my being baptized, and to be a part of our family again. She had since changed her name legally, in Tribal Court back to her birth name,

Karen Myrtle Black, which is the name she was born into and she carried proudly.

Christmas Eve 2012: I was spending the evening with my daughter, her husband and my grandchildren when my phone rang. It was my half brother, he said that he was at my mother's apartment and that I needed to come, that as the eldest sibling the coroner was waiting for me to positively ID my mother's body. The coroner assumed that she been gone for close to a week when my brother was able to get into her apartment. The assumption on her death certificate was that she had died of an accidental overdose as she was prescribed high doses of morphine for her chronic back pain.

I believe that my mother passed away from *Cultural Genocide*. I believe my mother's mind and spirit never healed from the atrocities that she suffered as a young girl. I believe that my mother's spirit was disconnected and was never returned to her People. I believe that my mother died because she was stolen from her mother, ripped from her community and shared like a state commodity in the welfare system. I believe that my mother died of her Indian being sick and wandering in two worlds but was disconnected from them both.

With the event of her passing I became adamant about doing research to reconnect with my family at Quinault/Quileute knowing that this is where she'd been stolen from. Knowing that this is where my matriarchal line was. I was searching for some closure of something that my mother was never able to heal from, looking for a way to honor the things that she and my grandmother had endured.

And so began my search for the rest of my disconnected family. This research I was soon to find out, was to be riddled with dead ends, road blocks and obstacles put in place by the Bureau of Indian Affairs to keep us disconnected from our people and our tribal communities. Although Washington State passed legislation in 2014 that allows adoptees access to their pre-adoption birth certificates, which I immediately applied for, for Indigenous peoples this still proves prob-lematic. Even though I now have my unaltered birth certificate, it lists my mother's ADOPTED name on it. This of course, is NOT her real name... because HER birth certificate was altered when she was abducted by the State and relocated to Oregon.

The more investigating that I've done, I find that it was very com-mon for adoptive families to force the Indian children whom they had adopted during the Scoop Era to relinquish their own children that were born to them, especially if they were underage, which then seals the fate of two generations of records within many families. But I remained hopeful and applied to Washington State Vital Sta-tistics for a copy of my mother's unaltered birth certificate. I was denied, and eventually went up the chain of command to be told, if I could obtain a tribal court order, "maybe" they would provide a copy of her original birth certificate, even though I had proof within my own unaltered birth certificate that she was indeed my biological mother.

I went immediately to Tribal Court and filed for a court order. The judge read my request and within that day granted me the order citing that "Karen Myrtle Black, child who was removed from the Quinault Indian Nation and her family during a period when such removals were made without proper consideration of the best inter-est of native children, their families and their tribes, NOW, THERE-FORE, IT IS HEREBY ORDERED that any governmental records available for Karen Myrtle Black, including her original birth certifi-cate, be made available to Rebecca Larsen." Dated January 26th, 2015.

I sent this Court Order to the state of Washington Vital Statistics, with a new request for a copy of my mother's unaltered birth certifi-cate, which they have yet again denied. This time citing that they have opened my mother's records and that they are sealed federally because of the era and the fact that she was Native American. In order to get a copy of her records I must now obtain a Court Order from King County Superior Court, only with this will they release any of her records to me. Where is our Nation to Nation sovereign and inherent relationship with the State of Washington?

So I began the struggle with my own Nation of my birth and my Ancestors, as well as the State of Washington. The Quinault Nation has also has proven to be very uncooperative in this process, hiding behind the policy that I have no rights to my own matriarchal family tree records discriminating against me, basically, because I am adopted. I have the proof in hand, I have a copy of my mother's birth certificate, I have a copy of her death certificate, I have a copy of my pre-adoption birth certificate which clearly lists my mother (with her adopted name) and I even have a letter dated in 1988 from the Bureau of Indian Affairs Confidential Records office stating they sent my mother's records to Quinault, listing her being born to Myrtle Black, April 11th, 1947.

One of the important factors to note is that I am not a "provisional" tribal member, I am not an "adopted" tribal member, I am fully enrolled Quinault Indian Nation woman, as was my mother, so in essence, Quinault policy of denying me my family tree, discriminates against us as women who were stolen from them and disconnected from our tribal community, in a way that they do not discriminate against anyone else who is a fully enrolled tribal member. I'm not seeking enrollment with this paperwork. I'm seeking the history of my matriarchal family line, which they continue to deny me.

Becky, 2016

As of this writing, at this time I do not know the outcome of what that may look like, or if policy may be shifted or changed because of my refusal to go away. I testified before the Tribal Council in February 2015 and walked away with very little hope of there being any real policy change. This lip service was paid because the QIN President at the time, invited me to come speak about the issue of cultural genocide to the Business council, where she feigned disbelief and stated to all present she did not know what the "Scoop" was or how it might have effected those that she serves in her capacity as our Nation's President.

I do not know what the outcome of any of this will be but I will continue this fight for all us as Unceded Children of Indigenous Nations, for all that we have had to endure. I will continue to this fight for open records in honor of my mother and because of what she and my grandmother had to suffer at the hands of the State and the Bureau of Indian Affairs. I will continue to fight for all of us who were stolen until we are welcomed back to our Homelands and to our People.

As is the tradition of our People, I now have a responsibility to carry this story and to speak my truth. We, as a People and as Nations, need to be standing in the truth of what the "Scoop" has done to our communities and to our families, of the historical trauma added to yet another generation of our People. I will not quietly fade away until I receive what is rightfully mine and I know that my mother and ALL the Grandmother's of my line stand with me. I will not be silenced, **until we bring our stolen children home.**

My friend shared this: "It's a song I hear on the beaches of the west coast: Ozette, Giants Graveyard, Point Grenville (where our old Quinault Long House used to sit.) These are the sites of the villages of the past. Before the New World. I hear the souls sing, and this is what I hear…

I listen to your soul
We all walk in a manner of looking for place of identity

to define our honor of our spirit
The Song of no place to go
They have taken everything
I have no place to pray
I have no place to cry
Please help me find who I am..." —*Phillip Ashue*

Becky Larsen made a moving YOU TUBE video.
https://www.youtube.com/watch?v=KxbodWnFxM4

5

Seeing in Color

Debra Newman (Choctaw Cherokee)

I am an adoptee of Choctaw, Cherokee, Scot and English decent. My adoptive parents began telling me very early that I was adopted. Throughout the years they always said the same thing, "Your mother couldn't take care of you, so she gave you to us." That was all the explanation I needed as a child.

My adoptive parents loved me completely and unconditionally and I returned their love in kind. Mom and Dad were wonderful 'salt of the earth' people. They have both walked on and I miss them daily. The most important thing in their lives was service to God, followed by their love for each other and then their four adopted children. My adopted siblings were much older than I and all left home by the time I was eight years old. This was fine with me because I finally had Mom and Dad all to myself! Mom was a home-maker and Dad worked at several different occupations, most of them at the same time. Dad was a natural teacher and one of the most patient people I have ever known. He taught high school science and math for nearly 30 years, as well as teaching both adult and children's classes in our church. He also farmed, ran a home improvement busi-ness and was a civil defense officer for several years. If there was a job he could do to help those around him, he did it gladly. Mom taught me to read very early and I was reading at a 4th grade level when I was three years old. She also taught me sewing. I can still make vir-tually anything. She was an excellent cook and I still use many of her recipes today. She rocked me to sleep every night and I still have that rocking chair. I feel her love every time I sit in it.

We lived on a farm and grew most of our own food. There were two huge gardens and numerous animals including cattle, chickens, goats, horses, dogs and a few dozen barn cats. My chores included caring for the animals, which was a job I truly loved. I spent as much time with them as I could. They were my playmates and dearly loved friends. In the summer I would often spend entire days riding my horse Brownie with no saddle or bridle. Tugging his mane in the direction I wanted him to go was all that was needed.

We took car trips to Long Beach, California every couple of years to visit my maternal grandparents. On the trip we took when I was three years old, we saw a pow wow in progress while traveling through the southwest. We stopped, and while enjoying the sights and sounds of the pow wow, a Native woman picked me up and took off with me. Mom did her best to follow her and Dad looked for someone to help. When security caught up to the woman, she was still unwilling to give me up. When security asked her why she was doing this, she told them in her own language that she didn't think the white people should have an Indian child. I have no memory of the abduction, but mom told me I never cried when the woman took me. I only cried when I saw Mom again, and the woman wouldn't let me go to her.

After that trip, I frequently took out our encyclopedia that covered American Indians and sat in front of a full length mirror, alternately looking at the pictures and then at myself. This went on for years and I wore that book out. I knew I was one of them even though mom told me I wasn't. I believe she honestly didn't realize she had a mixed blood Indian daughter.

School years were both good and bad. My favorite subjects were science and art and I still enjoy them today. I did very well in school and was well liked by the teachers. Many of them described me as "the girl who is always smiling." Getting along with the other children was a different matter entirely. It was quickly apparent that I did not fit in with the other children. I was never popular, but I had a couple of good friends. Going to art school was a new beginning. I got to start all over and learned to make friends and enjoy the company of other young people.

Growing up I knew I was lucky to have good parents, but I felt something important was missing. Sometimes, I wondered if I had a twin somewhere. I felt not quite complete, like half a person, or as if there was a large hole in myself. I felt as if I was playing a part in a lifetime play. Always pretending that this was me and my life, but the part never exactly fit. This feeling continued unabated until I was fifty years old. Fifty years is a very long time to wonder what was wrong with me and why I felt so different. It was a long time to wonder who on earth I was and where had I come from? Did I have any brothers and sisters? Did I look like anyone else in the world? Where did I get my artistic talent? Why did I feel a closer connection to animals and nature than others seemed too? Why did spirituality and the Creator seem so important to me? Why did I feel like I was being led or watched over by something I couldn't name? Was it God? If so, why me? So many questions with no answers for so very long.

Since I loved my parents deeply, and perhaps more importantly because they loved me, I decided the answers to these questions could wait until they passed on. I did not want to hurt them in any way. After they walked on, I was extremely lonely and alone in the world. I was not close to my adopted siblings, I had no husband or children. I developed numerous health problems that I later found out were manifestations of acute anxiety. I realized that never again would there be someone who put me ahead of themselves. When Dad died, the last person on earth who loved me was gone. It is a very lonely situation.

Nearly three years after Dad walked on, I could no longer wait to look for answers to my questions. It seemed reasonable that I might have a brother or sister somewhere and I decided to look for them. When I was seventeen, mom told me the name of my birth mother. Thirty-three years later I hoped I was remembering it correctly. It was my only lead. On Monday October 27, 2008, I began my search. I remembered a family-owned business in my hometown with the same last name as my birthmother's. I emailed them and told them I was looking for people who knew her. To my surprise they emailed back with the message that they knew exactly who I was talking about. They included a phone number for someone they said knew her family. I had to wait until after work to call the number and that was a very long day. I could not concentrate on work because of the endless possibilities that crowded my mind. Fortunately, my director at work was sympathetic and was very excited for me as well.

Finally at long last, the work day ended. I was too nervous to eat anything that day and my heart was racing with excitement and anticipation. Telling myself to be brave and calm, I dialed the number. A man answered and I told him who I was and what I wanted to know. He turned out to be a cousin by marriage and was very kind and patient with me. He began by telling me about my brother Bill. I had a brother! I was overjoyed. I was no longer alone on the world! I would have been completely happy with that, but before I could process the news, he was telling me about my sister Bonnie. I had a brother and a sister! A large pile of tissues was beginning to accumulate because I could not stop crying for the joy of knowing I had family. My dreams were coming true. I thought that was going to be it, but then I heard about siblings Lloyd, Joe Ann, Dixie, Shirley, Jimmy and Marvina! Could it possibly be true that I had eight brothers and sisters? No wonder I had always felt like part of myself was missing. I had a great big family and somehow my heart knew it and longed for them all these years.

Amazingly, most of the siblings lived in and around my hometown. He provided me with phone numbers for most of them and then told me, "Your mother is out in the nursing home." Time seemed to stop dead and I was completely speechless. Years before I had read that a woman with her name had died in 1974 in my hometown. Could it be that she was still alive when all these years I thought she was dead? He said that yes, she was still alive, but she was not in good health.

In one day, I had gone from having no one in the world to finding eight brothers and sisters and a mother! This was nearly too much to comprehend.

I was numb and astounded at the same time. What should I do now? Call one of the numbers he had given me or wait? I was terrified of rejection, so I considered not calling anyone that night. The need to connect with my blood was strong though and with equal parts excitement and fear I dialed Bill's number. I got the answering machine the first couple of calls and hung up. Then, I tried a third time and left a message. Shortly, a woman Kay called back and then Bill got on the extension. I don't remember much about the conversation. I was trying to process the fact that I was talking to my oldest brother just hours after beginning my search.

After getting off the phone with Bill, I was to excited to sleep and decided to call my sister Dixie. She had been sleeping when I called.

It took her a bit to wake up and understand what I was telling her. At first, she seemed like she didn't believe me. Then she suddenly remembered something and her whole attitude changed. She told me that when she was in grade school her class had gone to the New-man farm to pick pumpkins for Halloween. When they were done, all the children were invited inside to have refreshments. All except Dixie. The teacher made her sit on the bus by herself and she wasn't allowed to have anything. She was sitting there wondering what she had done wrong when she saw a tiny black haired girl waving at her from the open doorway. Dixie waved back and then a woman pulled the little girl inside and shut the door. The little girl, of course, was me. Dixie finally had an answer to why she wasn't allowed inside that day. She was my sister and the adults did not want us to see each other.

We were both very excited and knew we had to meet soon. I suggested the following Saturday, November 1, 2008. She said yes and she would let the other family members know. Understandably, I did not sleep much that night. After fifty long years I was going to meet my family and find out who I really was!

Saturday finally arrived and I was up early preparing for the trip back to my hometown. The drive afforded plenty of time to think about what lay before me. I knew this would be a day I would never forget and for better or worse it would change my life forever.

Dixie had reserved the party room of a local restaurant for us to meet and get acquainted. Arriving at the restaurant, I parked the car and sat there for a few moments. My new life lay inside that restaurant. I knew nothing would ever be the same. I asked the Creator to please make this a joyful day, took a deep breath and walked inside. The party room had glass walls and I saw there was only one person there. Our eyes met and held as I walked across the room to her. We had a long hug and stood looking at each other. It suddenly occurred to me that I had no idea which sister I was hugging! It was Dixie. For the first time, I was looking at a face which looked much like my own. Instantly, I felt a bit more complete. That hole in myself had gotten a little smaller. This was just the beginning. As we chatted, others started to arrive. I met most of my brothers and sisters that day, as well as brothers and sisters in law, nieces, nephews and their spouses. Each time I met someone new I felt an odd feeling in my chest, as if my heart grew larger with each meeting. We spent hours there, looking at old photos and learning about each other. It felt so very good. I never wanted it to end.

After a few hours, it was suggested that I write a letter to my mother. I did not expect to meet her that day and this was my opportunity to have some contact with her. One of the nieces took the letter to her and then called to say she wanted to meet me. I started to cry as much from happiness as fear. Some of the family and I drove over to her apartment. Driving there, going in the building, getting in the elevator and walking down the hall seemed as if they were happening to someone else entirely. I was simply a spectator along for the ride. The day was so full already, I wasn't sure about this and what might come from the meeting. I was truly terrified, more so than I'd ever been in my life.

When we got to her door, it was open a bit and fairly dark inside. Entering, I saw a tiny 89-year-old woman standing in the kitchen. I walked up and hugged her gently but firmly. She said, "You're not married." This stuck me as an odd thing to say when meeting for the first time, so I started to laugh and felt less scared about how this was going to turn out. She sat in her favorite chair and we talked a while. Then I noticed her hands. Tiny little delicate nine-year-old girl size hands, just like mine. I put my hand up, palm toward her and she put hers to mine. Our hands matched exactly. One older, one younger, but every part exactly the same size. It may sound insignificant, but that moment answered a lot of questions I had wondered about for so very long.

Then I asked her the question. Why? Why was I put up for adoption? She said a woman from the county had come to the house and told her that if she did not put me up for adoption, the county would take all the other children away. My brother Bill later corroborated this, telling me he remembered that day very well.

The day was coming to an end and I had a long drive, so I hugged everyone and began the journey home, feeling happier than I had felt since I was a little child. I drove home feeling all the hugs, the laughter and the tears of the day. So many people. So many names to remember! So much history to begin knowing. I was literally finding myself.

I spent the holidays with my family and my next birthday shopping with my sisters. At one of the stores we visited something beautiful occurred. As we all entered the store, the clerk said, "You all must be sisters." For the first time a stranger recognized me as belonging to family simply by how I looked! Smiling, I realized another moment had occurred that made me part of something truly wonderful...Blood, Biology, Family.

My sweet little sister Marvina and I burned up a lot of cell phone minutes after that and we've bonded very well. She was a wealth of information and graciously spent up to 5 hours at a time filling me in on the last 50 years of our family. She told me she had known who I was for years and had even waited on me at a local restaurant! She said she wanted to tell me who she was, but was afraid of changing my life.

I visited my mother several times over the next year and a half, until she walked on at nearly 91 years old. I asked about her parents and grandparents, but she said she knew nothing about her parents early life or her grandparents at all. They would not talk about it. I could only wonder what had been so terrible that it wasn't even mentioned.

I learned a few things about my father. He was an older man who passed on when I was 21. He was mixed blood like my mother and a veteran of WWI. Bonnie honored me with a photo of him and his face can be seen in mine.

One day while looking up genealogy, I found a site called the First Nations Repatriation Institute and Sandra Whitehawk. The website says First Nations Repatriation Institute provides technical assistance, education; research and advocacy on the process of Truth, Healing and Reconciliation for the healing and return home of First Nations people impacted by foster care and adoption. This would change my life as well.

Being a mixed blood adoptee was a challenge growing up. Being a Native adoptee only compounded the challenge. Something inside me had longed for inclusion in my culture. Being an adoptee herself, Sandra knew that. On November 3, 2012, Dixie and I attended their annual pow wow in Minneapolis, Minnesota. Every effort was made to have all of us feel wanted. I came home from the pow wow feeling acceptance, support, inclusion, friendship and culture in ways I had only dreamed of for decades.

Today, I have daily contact with other Native adoptees. Our shared experience bonds us firmly to one another. I consider them not just friends, but brothers and sisters. I no longer wonder where I came from. I know I have family, I know I look like other people in the world and I know where my artistic talents come from. The hole in myself is nearly gone. I no longer suffer from acute anxiety and all the symptoms it brings.

When people ask me what it is like to have found family and culture, I tell them it's like seeing in black and white all my life, then one day I woke up seeing in color. Every aspect of life has taken on a tone, contrast, saturation and clarity I never knew existed. I continue to have frequent contact with brothers and sisters and am forever grateful for their love and acceptance. Yahkohke.

Debra Newman is an artist. You can find her work on Facebook: Debra Newman Art.

6

Joey Claude Chookomoolin

Joseph Henning (Cree)

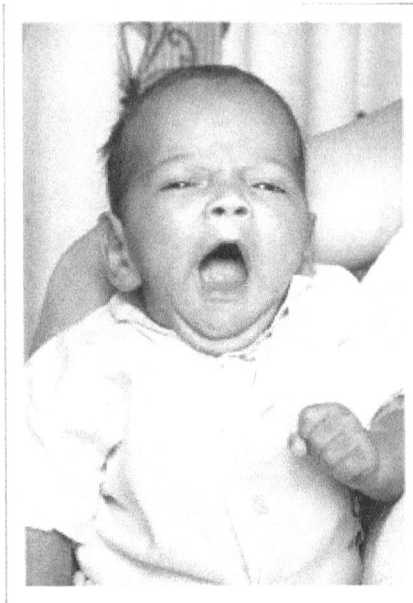

Baby photo, 1969. This was my 1st photo. I
was still in Canada and I'm guessing it was
the foster family holding me. They gave
these to my adopted mom.

After a few days and a few more attempts... let's try again. This is
after all kind of difficult to discuss. I'm almost sure whoever might be
reading this knows that already.

Well my name is Joe. I grew up on Long Island, New York. A
nice town called Dix Hills, located in Suffolk County. It was all I
knew growing up and that I was adopted. I was the only Native in
the area and even though it sounds bad, it wasn't. My adopted parents were white; my mother was Italian and my father was German.

I have an older adopted brother, Kevin, too. He is of Scandinavian descent, which I think is pretty cool… my brother "The Viking."

Our parents never hid the fact we were adopted. We both knew from an early age, and quite frankly we didn't care. In fact one of my earliest memories was being in a department store running around with him. He has seven years on me, so… I was a tag-along little brother. I can still remember the red and blue ball he gave me. It was one of those "get to meet your future brother meetings" in Toronto; I assume that now.

I wasn't even adopted yet.

Strange how I can remember that but nothing else.

I have no memories of my foster parents or anything else from Canada… except that meeting. I know that this family cared for me because years later my mother showed me the letters the foster family wrote for them about my routines, care, dislikes and likes. It felt weird reading those the first time. I still to this day wonder about them. They had me for over a year. But soon I was adopted and crossed the border from Canada to the USA. I never saw the foster parents again or gave it much thought until my teens.

Like every family we had our problems and I guess I was a wee bit insecure. I remember having an argument with my parents and yelling, "Why don't you ship me back to where you adopted me from if you're unhappy with my behavior!" My dad, being who he was, told my mom to get a box big enough… I think I got my sarcasm from him. It was soon after that my mom showed me those letters. She told me they were just the foster parents. She had no idea who my birth parents were or why I was given up. Just that she and dad loved me to bring me to their home and wanted to make me part of their family.

Being young and wondering of my past, I looked for more information. I asked mom and all she knew I was an Indian: an

Ottawapiskat Indian was all she was told. (Found out years later how it was misspelled so I told her. It's Attawapiskat, not Ottawapiskat.) I looked more and found out I was adopted out of the Angel Guardian Home. When I was around age 14 or 15, I called the adoption agency. They told me my parents died in an auto accident. Maybe they told me that to stop me from calling again but I never forgot that. I called quite a few times asking for information on my heritage and such, but always got told they weren't able to tell me. My guess is they finally got sick of me calling and told me my parents died in an auto accident... End of story. I stopped looking.

Needless to say that hurt like hell. It made me feel more alone and I guess that it had the desired effect. I stopped calling them and made due with what I had. But it never really filled that void I had: my feeling of separation and being one of a kind. A few close friends called me "Last Brave Standing" as a joke and as a sign they understood. Being the only Indian (Native now) with long hair was pretty cool, but again it never fixed the way I felt about myself.

It was back in the early 1990s, I'd heard of "The Missing Children" on *Unsolved Mysteries*. I was sleeping and my girlfriend woke me saying I have to watch this. It explained that during the 1960s, thousands of Native children were taken without explanation and adopted out. I started shaking; I wrote down the info from the show but never heard back. It was a repeat but I never forgot it. We both knew back than I was Native, I was adopted, I came from Canada. That was all.

I asked my mom how my adoption was done. She went to an agency in New York and they found me. She knew nothing else. So again I was at a dead end. I never forgot what they told me when I was younger and didn't even want to open those wounds again. So again I let it lie.

September 11, 2001: we all know that day. I was there, remember it all. It was also the beginning of a new journey. I had some problems with drinking so I went to rehab. To be completely honest I was required by court… yes, I screwed up big time due to my drinking. I was sent there for a year to work out the addiction. Being there you are required to be on welfare so the state picks up the tab. I lost my wallet. My social security card… everything gone. I had to re-apply for another card and that's when it all happened. I'm glad I was in treatment when it all came to light. I don't know how I would've handled things if I was drinking. Or even if I would.

I was told first I wasn't a US citizen. I was still Canadian and to get my SS card back, I'd have to get information about my past for them to see. Keep in mind I lost my information before and never had these problems but after 9/11 they got a lot stricter. My mom helped find all the records pertaining to my adoption, when I crossed the border and everything else. It was also the first time I saw my last name at birth. Well, after countless trips to Manhattan to the federal building, it got cleared up and I got a resident card. It was then my curiosity kicked in with my birth name.

I went to the public library to google it. Found a bunch of names and came across a weird bunch of numbers and letters. (Turns out they were a Canadian zipcodes.) So being not too "tech savvy," I asked the librarian for help. She asked what I was looking for so to begin I told her part of my birth name and she asked if I might be *Joey Claude Chookomoolin.* She gave me a birth date and it was a day off, but it was right. She told me than I was being searched for.

I couldn't breathe. I was shocked, who?

Turns out the internet page was for Adoptees being searched for… the Canadian Adoptees Registrar: Birth Relatives Searching: Year 1968. I was there, after marked "FOUND," then removed. I long since forgot that group of finders, I wish I remembered so I could thank them again.

I had a sister searching for me. She posted that awhile back and she had moved a few times since the posting. I was given the phone number first for the website though. This is where I was glad to be in treatment. I went right to my counselor and explained what just happened. I was shaking. I was scared. I was angry.

Angel Guardian Home told me I had no one. My parents had died. So who was looking? Together we called the site. I gave them the information for me and was told I have a sister. She's been searching for quite some time. Would I be interested in talking to her? Stupid question I thought. Why would I be calling if I wasn't?

Anyway in a few hours I got a call saying they contacted her and here is a number or here is my number for contact. I forget but within a few more hours I was talking to my sister Trish. She told me she looked for years especially because mom was still crying each Mother's Day.

Mom???…. I was shocked. I started crying. I thought she was dead for years and now I find out she is alive and I have two sisters and a brother on her side. In a few minutes, I was talking to her. We all were crying at that point. I was so happy to know finally. We talked and promised to keep in touch. It was also when I first heard of the Residential Schools. One of the reasons why my adoption took place. I searched online and printed up pages of testimony about those places and got sick… really sick. Again one reason why I was glad for the treatment… I shared it with them first. The horrors that took place there just 30 years before. I was enraged to think my mom and dad endured this treatment. I cried, I screamed and punched more than a few holes in the walls thinking about it. How dare they do that!

Now for the hard part. How to tell (adoptive) mom I found them. Would she be mad? Sad I wanted them more maybe? Would she think I betrayed her? Besides that how would she take the fact of what happened in Canada at that time? I finally went home and told her. She cried with me. She held me and told me she wasn't mad. She was happy I found them. When we talked of the Residential Schools, she lost it though. My mom was a devout Catholic. For her to know it was the church to commit these acts, it broke something. I still regret telling her that part. She cried in private as she read the reports I printed. She asked what I wanted to do. I asked would she mind if I went up there for a visit to meet them. After those words came out, her purse and keys were in her hand. "C'mon, we got to get some things." She took me shopping for my trip to Canada. I still think she thought I was going to the Arctic because she bought Polar Stuff. Still laugh to this day about that… that was my mom.

Anyway my trip was a surprise. My sister and step dad knew but that's it. I took the bus up. My mom dropped me off and said she'd be there when I returned. I had a layover in Toronto. My first trip there since my adoption. That's another story in itself. But when my sister told me that Timmins was the largest city north of Toronto, I was expecting a "city" city, not what I found. Funny. But walking through that door and seeing my mom doing the dishes is one of the things I'll never forget. We both cried. Ron, my step dad, who I did call dad, told me each night I slept, she'd be watching me. The Mother's Day thing I mentioned earlier…. I was born May 12th. Right around Mother's Day that year. After I was born they took me. They never let her see me or hold me. All she got was a flower in a vase when she woke up, saying "It's a boy. Congratulations." That was all. They told her being she was 17 ½, she'd have to wait until her 18th birthday and married to get me back. At 18 she was married to Ron, stable job and home, and they went to get me. It was then she was told I was already adopted. It broke her heart. So every Mother's Day, she'd lock herself in her room and cry. Trish told me that was the inspiration for her to search for me.

During that trip I got to meet my aunts from my father's side. He lived on a reserve north of Timmins and we'd go up there to see him if I wanted. We did. A train ride and a very long truck ride on a winter road until we reached Fort Albany. I got to meet my Grandparents, too. Wonderful people and my grandma cried, saying, "welcome home." Turns out I was their first kid for the both of them. (The oldest but not the wisest.)

(As I'm writing it may seem matter of fact or cold. I'm trying not to cry right now. It's difficult but I'm doing it so bear with me)

I stayed up in Canada for quite some time before returning home to the US. I told mom of my trip and everyone there. My families from both sides. How the trip went to the reserve. Meeting my grandparents. She was happy for me.

Like I said at the beginning, all families have problems. At 15 I lost my (adoptive) dad to cancer. I didn't take it well and became very self-destructive. I felt guilty and angry about that. You see when my dad got sick, I ran away. I stayed away until it was too late and the last time I spoke to him, he didn't even know who I was. My mom knew that. She knew that really hurt me so she did something in time that I still cannot forget.

She kept asking me if I planned on returning to Canada. She knew I thought about doing that but I didn't want to leave her. She told me I should. Go now and live where I was meant to. She had the beginnings of Alzheimer's and she wanted me to go before it got too bad. She made me promise when I go, not to return. To remember her like she was. Because she might not remember me and she knew how devastated I was after my dad died. I cannot think of how she was able to be so strong. I did. I left…. We talked every Sunday until she couldn't talk no more. We said our farewells one last time. God I miss her. I kept my promise.

Joe hugs his mom first time

I'm glad she passed now because if she knew about the 60s Scoop, she would feel even worse.

Had to stop for a bit… got emotional here.

Anyway here I am now living in Attawapiskat, my mom's reserve. Been here for over 10 years now on reserve in Canada since 2004.

My name is Joseph M. Henning/Joey Claude Chookomoolin.

My mom is Alexina Clement now. My Dad is Augustine Scott.

My mom's side, I have two sisters, Trish and Carolyn and a brother, Ernie.

My dad's side. Well let's see: Joanne, Ruth, Boy, Angel and quite a few others.

Cousins all over, a few I keep in contact with, a few I know and a few I never even met.

Back in the states, I have my brother Kevin. A wonderful sister in law Dianne, an awesome nephew and niece, Danny and Jaclyn.

My ex-wife with our daughter Jessica who I miss dearly and 3 wonderful step kids who will always be my kids in my heart, Joey, Anthony and Melissa.

I'm with a wonderful woman who is from this reserve and we have a two-year-old boy named Clark Peter Tookate Henning. He got the middle name after his grandfather Peter. He was a wonderful man and I'm glad he got to see Clark.

It's still hard for me here though. I still don't fit in. I do not speak Cree, a few words but that's it. I know nothing of our culture, our history. I'm what some here call an apple. I'm red on the outside and white in the inside. They're right. The 60s Scoop did the job it was supposed to. I'm not white, I'm not Native, but I'm learning. That's why my son will grow up here. To be Native and live it. I'll show him my world in time but now it's for us both to learn what we are, to grow.

My moms side, my two sisters and nieces.

There is always hope no matter how dark things get. As long as I have an open heart and mind, anything is possible. Blood bonds us all.

For those looking for home or lost/stolen family, there is hope. I found my way. Never give up hope. I didn't plan on this journey. It just happened. I didn't plan on writing this either. But here I am. Everything in life happens for a reason. We are given a journey and we will survive. We will learn. We will return home.

*I was in Foster care until I was 18 months! I didn't go into the states till 1970/71! They lied to her and me years later.

I told my story for my mother. On April 12 2016, Alexina Clement (Chookomoolin) passed away. Forever in my heart, mom. I'm glad for the time we had and your son did return home.

Me, my wife/common law Violet and our
son Clark.

7

The Affair

Janelle Black Owl (Mandan, Hidatasa, Turtle Mountain Chippewa, Lakota)

This was written when I finally had a full understanding of what happened and from the adoption file that I obtained from the state. My birth mother and father had an affair. He was married and had my two brothers already. My mother was married and had my sisters. Her husband was in jail at the time of the affair and my birth. He could not and would accept me. I was one year old when he came home and apparently he was very abusive and would have anything to do with me and take no responsibility for me. My sister told me that the social worker came and got me just before Christmas. According to the adoption file, I was removed from my family on December 1. My Mother made a choice and I was not it.

She chose him

instead of me

She loved him

and wanted him

more than me

Long before I came along

he was hers

and she was his there

was no way

they would let

me

ruin their love

their loved remained

and I was thrown away

her love for me

did not matter

the love I was

supposed to have for her

did not matter

their love

was all that did

I hated him

when I should have

hated her too

Now I just hate me

because I did not matter.

I hated this man for YEARS and thought I would kill him
when I saw him. But the man I met was a very pitiful
person. I shook his hand and said, "Nice to meet you, uncle"
and in THAT moment, everything I felt for him went away
and I literally felt nothing.

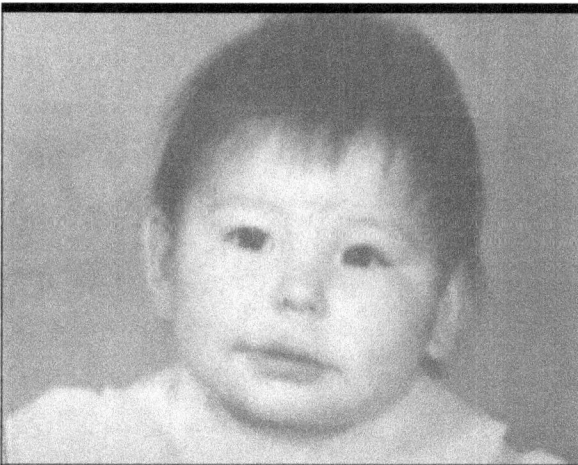

Janell, not quite one year old

I never had the "fairy tale dream" about what I wanted to find when I began my search for my biological family. I never had expectations whatsoever. I just knew that before I moved on with my life, I had to try and find them, and whatever I came across, I would deal with. I never really fantasized about them growing up, but I did wonder about them.

I was 19 when I found them, 20 when I met them, and by the time I was 22 things had gone from good to awkward to weird to bad to OK.

I had found my bio mother and her family first. When I first talked to her she told me that woman I had initially contacted was actually my sister/cousin from bio fathers side. FATHER? WHAT? Up until that point I never gave that much thought about him, because I assumed he would just not be part of the picture. Bonus for me, I had found both sides of my family in one phone call.

Because I had lived with my birth mother for the first year of my life, they all knew about me. So in this family when I came back, that was it. I was back in the family. People told me they had been praying for me to come back, they had known about me and that I was not a secret. Well, that changed things for me. I was glad that they knew and it took away years of loneliness I felt because I thought no one cared, then I wondered why no one ever tried to look for me. Then I was confused and hurt. I got to know so many of my family and I am so fortunate that I did because now many of them are gone. I was never very close to any of this side of my family except for a few. Me and my mother went over many times about why she did what she did. I never fully understood it, because she never fully explained it. Because of choices she made in her life I was just never close to her. There are those one I have kept in touch with over the years, but sporadically and some I am still getting to know.

I still have contact with her, but never directly. It is always through one of my siblings. I just can't talk directly with her.

When I connected with my bio fathers side of the family, that was a little more difficult because they did not know. The sister/cousin that I had contacted initially had told her mom and they were the only two that had known because from what they told me, he had had them look for me once. I went to go meet them and got to know a lot of family.

Both reunions were so different. Both were uncomfortable, because even though I knew I was family by blood, I was an outsider, and that was made very clear very quickly. But I felt complete. I met my family I saw people I looked like and I finally began to get the story of why they chose not keep me. That was what I need to know. What happened.

My mother and father had had an affair and here I am is what happened. My mother kept me for a year, then decided to chose her husband over me and gave me up. He was not accepting of me at all and very abusive to all of us. So, this was not a bad choice.

I had a good reunion with both sides of my family. They all accepted me and loved me with open arms and allowed me to come into their world and get to know who I was. But it did not stay that way. As life goes and I developed relationships with people it changed. I asked my birthfather his side of the story and I matched what my mother had said, but when I said he had an affair with my mother that upset him. My brother is six months older than me so there really is no denying it. He simply did not like the way I was talking to him and asking him questions, but I felt like I had a right to know because it was my life. He was a very quiet man and not very forthcoming with some information. I was too open and honest and that just didn't seem to work. Plus other people got involved, and I knew that because they did not know me, they would back up their relative. So our relationship changed drastically. But I had fabulous relationships with so many other people from that side of my family and to this day, I still do. It got to the point where I no longer spoke to my birthfather until he was on his death bed. We were able to make peace with one another at that time. I am thankful that I got to meet him, and know him what little bit I did.

I have no regrets about my search. I know who I am. I know my family. I have had great relationships with some, and some not so great relationships. Some just never existed. I still keep in contact with both sides of my family but only with the people who can just accept me for me. When I went and searched, I was looking for me. It was a long hard process but I finally did, and have accepted me for who I am with everything that made me, and I am OK with all of it.

I know that I am very fortunate to have found my birth mother and birth father and so many relatives from both sides of my family. Many adoptees do not. It has not been easy, but it has been beautiful.

I am who I am because of them, and despite them.

March 11, 2016
Since I wrote this piece, my birth mother has since passed away. It has been very weird. My six sisters and my aunty's and extended family, have embraced me in a way they have not since I found them so long ago. It has been a blessing. I decided not to go home for my mother's funeral. I decided that a long time ago. At my father's funeral, my sister and my friend had to walk me out of the building because I stood by his casket and broke down in such a way I never thought I would. My heart was broken because I did not know the man who laid before me in the casket the way my relatives did. He was very kind and loving to them, and I am so happy for them that he was so special to all of them. I wished I had known him that way. I did not want to go through the same thing with my mother. But the fact that my family remembered me and included me, and checked on me daily during that time, meant so much. She too, was very special to many people and loved. I am happy for those who knew her that way.

My heart is hurt because I did not know my birth parents in a different way. But without them, I would not be here. It is very weird to realize that I am all that's left of them, together. They blessed me by giving me life. They hurt me because they did not value my life. They loved me as best they could. I learned to love me despite them and because they helped make me the woman I am today. Without them, I would be right back where I started…as nothing.

Janelle contributed an essay CAUGHT IN THE MIDDLE, in the anthology CALLED HOME: Lost Children of the Indian Adoption Projects (2014), published by Blue Hand Books.

8

To Us You Belong (RAD Aftermath)

Levi William EagleFeather Sr. (Sicangu Lakota)

Living life for me during my early years was much like walking through a very color-full yet very surreal collage of everyone else's bad or left-over dreams. Nothing made any sense! Hello, my name is Levi William EagleFeather Sr. I am a Lakota by heritage. Sicangu Lakota by birth. I am an enrolled member of the Rosebud Sioux tribe of Rosebud South Dakota.

I was adopted at the age of four but haven't been since I changed my mind about it at the age of 15 and got the hell away from the whole sordid mess.

That was quite awhile ago. I'm 55 now.

It wasn't until the first summer I sundanced that those dreams faded and reality became mine. Clarity, like cool clear water to a thirsty parched throat or shade to a sun-drenched overheated mind, soothed my weary war-torn senses and underfed spirit. At long last I had found sanctuary and once again re-entered the land of the human being—or as we say in Lakota, *Ikce Wicasa (common man)*.

Somewhere in Scott Momaday's writing he wrote that telling a story takes words to describe words. Life is certainly that way. Whether it's yours or mine, it's story. Being such it requires or demands words many words to bring forth a full sense of our reality. Words which describe the full spectrum of thought, emotion and feeling that make-up the scattered and fragmented and sometimes incomprehensible reality of our lives as American Indians—especially in the aftermath of the wars and ongoing efforts of genocide against our people. Adoption is but one of those many efforts and the resulting ism's are but its results. Results that force us into, well let's just say that chameleons have nothing on us! Nevertheless, for sanity's sake, for peace of mind these results are ours to overcome.

The words of our overcoming, these words, my words, your words, our words describe just a portion of life's meaning, but it's our life and it's important. A living reality of experience, thought, feeling and emotion. No two experiences are ever exactly alike. No two thoughts, feelings or emotions are ever exactly the same, at the same time, or about the same thing. Always ongoing ever-changing, growing, *metamorphisizing* neither negative or positive necessarily, but always changing describing the ever shifting, ever adapting, overcoming that is life and living.

That part of life and living that in its many forms and shapes is you and me, the American Indian.

In looking back, when all is said and done, life has been pretty full for me, as it should be. I am, for the most part, most of the time, a happy man and enjoy living, come what may. Although, it hasn't always been this way. Time and distance have allowed my spirit the space needed to recover somewhat so the light of day no longer sears the consciousness of my soul. I think the experience of surviving hell and high water, and coming out on the other side, does that to a person. Living through it can and often does make us creatures of a darker understanding of life and living—sometimes morphing us into a breed of walking dead, soul dead.

Adoption can be like that, hell and high water, for some. It was for me and my sibs (siblings).

I realize throughout it all some don't do so well. Adapt and overcome I mean. Seems that some get burned pretty bad and take on lots of water and experience lots of hurting for many years after. I think, myself, I just became hell. Unfortunately, for those associated with me or those who experienced me during my early days will attest that that was the reality of being too close or trying to get to know me. There was much scorched earth left in the wake of my struggling. Struggling to survive those early years on my own alone.

Understanding the reality of all of this. Who, what and
why I was and am has taken many years to gather and digest.

One thing good about us though is that we are just another form of nature.

Being such, raw nature, we are energy.
Raw energy and we seek to flow.
In flowing we seek our own level much
like water running to the sea. Sometimes we rage
sometimes we flood
cutting our way through the rock and the barriers that
obstruct our knowing and our understanding.
Our journey our
destiny if you will becomes cluttered with the debris of our

raging and flooding. Disrupted journey's
disrupted destiny's
on the way to experience
the ebb and flow of natural being.

This writing was the first in a series I did. Words, just words strung together to convey meaning and understanding to a reality that wasn't supposed to exist, but it does. It's my story.

Life in general is pretty good most of the time. The rest of the time… well let's say there are situations we find ourselves in and experiences we find ourselves having to endure that color our sky grey and sometimes even black, with fear, doubt, insecurity, and aloneness.

Adoption or being adopted can be such a situation.

Back in the day, oh say, about forty years ago: when I woke up and started finding my way free of its grip. My life was ripe with fear, doubt and insecurity and yes, I was alone. In looking back on that time and the four decades since, it is clear to me now just what a mind fuck western society really is and how precious and important not only the philosophy, but the worldview and culture of my people are. Not only to me, but to succeeding generations of young who share in Lakota heritage and maybe even to others in the world who have lost connection to their ancestral past.

Having said that, I also realize how far behind the eight ball we, us Lakota's, are in general, as a people, in our ability to see beyond the destruction of our past in order to appreciate our present so we might look to the future. Such is the nature of death and dying. Grief takes time. Its own time! Not only to happen, but to happen appropriately so that when coming out on the other side our eyes are dry and clear seeing again. So that our hearts are right and strong!

Now this is not something that is waiting to happen. The grieving process, I mean. For my people the Lakota and for other nations of indigenous people, it is something that is happening and has been happening for quite some time. It is something that still is below the radar and understanding of the general public, maybe. I'm sure there is a reason for it if this is so.

Anyway, this overcoming is happening for individuals, as well, and has been happening for quite some time. American Indian folk who have experienced the adoption process are now gaining experience of overcoming the disconnections, the death and the dying of the old. Overcoming the grief and aloneness, of being separated from the herd, so to speak. It is a good thing to see and a good time to be alive!

In the more modern traditions of my people, part of the process of overcoming is referred to as the "Wiping of Tears." There are other parts to it also because grieving is a process. I am grateful for many and too many men and women of my Nation and other Nations of indigenous people. To those who have persevered through all that has happened and continue to persevere through that which is still happening to destroy us today. Not only for persevering through that which is set out to destroy our people as a whole, but also for understanding and seeing that which happens and is set out to destroy each of us as individuals.

Yes, there are those who help wherever and whenever they can as much as they can with all they have been given. Endlessly and tirelessly and sometimes at the expense of their own health and comfort. It is called sacrificing for others. The most notable of these folk in my life have a history of this kind of service to our people. They are Richard Moves Camp, Rick Two Dogs, Elmer Running, Roy Stone, and Ray Owens, all descended of Lakota and Dakota healers and spiritual leaders and healers and leaders themselves.

This same process (a microcosm of the larger) has been happening within the world of those who have undergone and survived adoption. Overcoming and "Wiping of Tears" has been and is happening. My journey began some four decades ago and continues today. While the overcoming is about finding belonging and becoming connected again, it is also about understanding how you belong and interacting positively with those to whom you belong. This takes a lifetime because it is what living is about!

For American Indian adoptees at its core, at least for now, it starts with searching out and finding our roots. Sadly, and I say this with tenderness and gentleness and caring in my heart and mind. Some may not be able to find that part of the knowing and understanding of reconnection that they seek. Be discouraged, but not too discouraged. Feel helpless because you do need help, lots of it!

> **DON'T FEEL TOTALLY HELPLESS THOUGH, BECAUSE YOU BELONG. YOU BELONG TO ME AND IN MANY WAYS TO EVERY PERSON WHO HAS EVER HAD THE MISFORTUNE TO HAVE UNDERGONE ADOPTION AND HAS EXPERIENCED BEING DISCONNECTED FROM THE SOURCE OF THEIR BEGINNING AND SURVIVED.**

Within this world, within this reality, our reality, there are many good, solid and strong folk too, though! Who are giving of themselves and of their lives in service to us. In pushing back against the mental, emotional, physical and spiritual pain and suffering that all too often comes with our situation and experiences. They have been put there of their own volition, yes, but also have spiritually answered a call for the sake of all. The most notable of folks whom I know in this situation, our situation, are Trace, author of books (like this one) and editor owner of the SplitFeathers Blog and other assorted groundbreaking actions of leadership; Sandy White Hawk, a fellow Sicangu Lakota and a leader in Adoptee issues and actions from the St Paul MN area; Susan Devan Harness, a university teacher, writer, involved with a Gazillion Voices Magazine along with other assorted efforts of overcoming; and to Robert DesJarlait, writer, artist, spokesperson on Indian issues and as always involved and knowledgeable on ICWA and most things related to caring and raising children as an Annishnabe Ogicheedag. These folk are out there, active and leading in their own way. To us, you belong.

So, this much is true for me! I've seen this and experienced this on my journey according to the cultural understanding and perspective of my reality as my life unfolds. Of course it is a spiritual journey now and has been for some time now. No longer cruising along according to the hegemony and discourse of western thought. While it is still our world, my world, it is now my interpretation of what is. In that vein of thought, I must confess western man is whacked out, has been all this time and we are the ones who remain sane. Staying within this world of sanity is my niche for now. I call it living through the reversing of the mind fuck!

Next, let's look within the realm of the most severe symptom of adopteeism: the status or label of *Reactive Attachment Disorder.*

The twentieth century has produced a world of conflicting visions, intense emotions, and unpredictable events, and the opportunities for grasping the substance of life have faded as the pace of activity has increased. Electronic media shuffle us through a myriad of experiences which would have baffled earlier generations and seem to produce in us a strange isolation from the reality of human history. Our heroes fade into mere personality, are consumed and forgotten, and we avidly seek more venues to express our humanity. Reflection is the most difficult of all our activities because we are no longer able to establish relative priorities from the multitude of sensations that engulf us. Times such as these seem to illuminate the classic expressions of eternal truths and great wisdom seems to stand out in the crowd of ordinary maxims. —*Vine Deloria Jr. (his preface to John Neihardts book "Black Elk Speaks)**

Reality can be such a bastard sometimes! Just when you think you got it nailed, something happens and it all slips away. Good fortune, its second cousin, seems to operate along these same lines! You work hard, you're ready, waiting, arms wide open and everything, then something happens blowing it all away. Does this sound familiar? Some people would say a person who thinks this way is just, "waiting for the axe to fall." And if you think this way, too much of the time, it becomes a self-fulfilling prophecy.

In medical terms, they say someone who thinks like this or sees life in this way is showing signs of paranoia. Meaning that someone is showing "a tendency….. toward excessive or irrational suspiciousness and distrustfulness of others." In some situations, this kind of thinking can develop into a more serious condition known as *schizophrenia*. Noah Webster says schizophrenia is "a psychotic disorder characterized by loss of contact with the environment, by noticeable deterioration in the level of functioning in everyday life, and by disintegration of personality expressed as disorder of feeling, thought (as delusions), perception (as hallucinations), and behavior—called also *dementia praecox*—compare paranoid schizophrenia."

Certain spiritually abusive things have happened to us American Indian people since western society brought its socially dysfunctional ways to our land.

All of these happenings have been inducing an isolating-oriented trauma on our people for several generations now. These things in particular, the wars, reservations, boarding schools, relocation programs and adoption. These things which have worked in harmony, one after the other or simultaneously together, pretty much shattering and destroying the ways in which the beauty and magnificence of who we are as human beings can be fully realized, understood and enjoyed. I would say at this point RAD was intentioned, and paranoid and schizophrenic type thinking and behavior are to be expected.

The people who started these practices against us, in the past and continue to practice them today, have gotten away with it and continue making money off of doing it. Maybe not directly anymore, but indirectly still and that's as simple and as good for them as it can get! It indicates success, at least to them, of their westernized way of doing things.

By agitating and manipulating the destruction of others, confiscation of birthrights and through carefully and systemically-applied abuses. These people have been capable, down through history of drastically changing tribal realities. Changing realities from systems which were built on self-reliance and were constructed for self-perpetuation to a single system which is built and designed solely for controlling and perpetuating the continued self-destruction of tribalism for profit. In short using you, your relatives and your friends, to educate and labor towards your own self-destruction.

> **If you think I'm wrong or misguided in my way of thinking, look and see who has all the land, all the say, and continues smiling all the way to the bank. We'll call this group the top layer of western society. It is a top down system and we'll call this layer the instigators or the 1% er's of western society. The shot callers, so to speak. There are other layers to this society. Here in America we know them as the middle, the lower, and the indigent classes. But for now I want to draw your attention to something else.**

A simple fact! Obscured quite possibly by our own cultural amnesia of our individual ancestral roots is the fact we knew this was coming.

A little less than 150 years ago my people, the Lakota, still understood our purpose. We knew and understood what sacrificing of ourselves was about. Of course, we still lived in Tipi's on the wide open prairie and still hunted buffalo and much more. But we also lived in a civilized manner as civilized human beings then too. We knew and understood how fragile yet necessary keeping good relationships were to our health and wellbeing. We also knew and understood the threat and danger western thought and living posed to our health and well-being. The inevitability of this threat coming to fruition came through in dreams and visions of some of our great leaders of that time. Black Elk, a healer, was one of those leaders.

Black Elk was born in 1863 and lived until 1950. He was born well before the time of either the Sioux or the American Indian. He was born and lived as a Lakota. He thought, reasoned and behaved according to the Lakota way of being. He lived his life, perceiving reality understanding it and speaking of it in the language from within the worldview of his time. The Lakota worldview.

In the summer of 1872 at the age of nine Black Elk experienced a vision. In 1930, through a translator, Black Elk related his experience to John Neihardt, who in turn wrote about it as, "The Great Vision" in his book *Black Elk Speaks*. Whether this vision came to him through intuition, spiritual insight, or from hearing reports of what was befalling our Dakota relatives to the east, Black Elk's vision was spot on. Experienced well before the reservation, boarding school, relocation, and adoption eras of our people it was a foretelling. A vision foretelling the, as yet, unforeseen problems of becoming westernized. Something that we now experience on the regular, day in and day out.

The following is an excerpt from this "The Great Vision:"

And as we went the voice behind me said: "Behold a good nation walking in a sacred manner in a good land!"

Then I looked up and saw that there were four ascents ahead, and these were generations I should know. Now we were on the first ascent and all the land was green. And as the long line climbed, all the old men and women raised their hands, palms forward, to the far sky yonder and began to croon a song together, and the sky ahead was filled with clouds of baby faces.

When we came to the end of the first ascent we camped in the sacred circle as before, and in the center stood the holy tree, and still about us was all green.

Then we started on the second ascent, marching as before, and still the land was green, but it was getting steeper. And as I looked ahead, the people changed into elks and bison and all four footed beings and even into fowls, all walking in a sacred manner on the good red road together. And I myself was a spotted eagle soaring over them. But just before we stopped to camp at the end of that ascent, all the marching animals grew restless and afraid that they were not what they had been, and began sending forth voices of trouble, calling to their chiefs. And when they camped at the end of that ascent, I looked down and saw that leaves were falling from the holy tree.

And the Voice said: "Behold your nation, and remember what your Six Grandfathers gave you, for thenceforth your people walk in difficulties."

Then the people broke camp again, and saw the black road before them towards where the sun goes down, and black clouds coming yonder; and they did not want to go but could not stay. And as they walked the third ascent, all the animals and fowls that were the people ran here and there, for each one seemed to have his own little vision that he followed and his own rules; and all over the universe I could hear the winds at war like wild beasts fighting.

And when we reached the summit of the third ascent and camped, the nation's hoop was broken like a ring of smoke that spreads and scatters and *the holy tree seemed dying and all its birds were gone. And when I looked ahead I saw that the fourth ascent would be terrible.*

Then when the people were getting ready to begin the fourth ascent, the Voice spoke like someone weeping, and it said: "Look there upon your nation." And when I looked down, the people were all changed back to human, and they were thin, their faces sharp, for they were starving. Their ponies were only hide and bones and the holy tree was gone.

At this point Black Elk remarked: "I think we are near that place now, and I am afraid something very bad is going to happen all over the world." He cannot read and knows nothing of world affairs. *

Levi in 2016

Adoption causes RAD and RAD is a more normal reaction to adoption than not. Adoption in western society, especially the transracial adoption of American Indian children was and is an unnecessary and unnatural situation. Historically, the process of taking American Indian children away from families who birth them, love them, view them and understood them as their future causes immense suffering and loss that reverberates and is felt throughout each one of our nations. It broke our sacred hoop keeping the beauty of life just out of arms reach or so it seems.

The destruction didn't happen overnight of course. Each and every one of these abuses aimed at destroying us was applied incrementally, generation after generation. Each and every one of them has done a pretty good job at what it was intended, and it isn't over yet. It happened, some of it is still happening, and there isn't a whole lot we can do to stop it at this point. At least, I don't know of anything I can do that will.

This is not the reason I started writing this, however. To talk endlessly about the things I cannot do or cannot change. The past is the past and there isn't much we can do about that. Blaming won't help, blaming ourselves and each other definitely won't, but by being responsible and holding ourselves and each other accountable for recourse and recovery can.

As depressing as this writing all sounded, it was! I now prefer to spend the majority of my time working against the effects it has had on the hearts and minds of our people. So this will be the last I will have to say about all of that.

I've been working against the negative effects our past has had on us for the past thirty five years or so. Both personally in my own life and the lives of my family members. As well as, professionally and as a volunteer within the American Indian community. Whenever the opportunity arose wherever it was I might have happened to be living at the time. Most recently I was able to offer my programming abroad, as a side job, amongst the folk in Germany, whenever the opportunity would arise.

I started out slowly of course way back then with baby steps. Thirty five years have gone by and I seem to be walking much better now. On good days I think I might even be able to walk and chew gum. We shall see.

In my next series of blog articles at American Indian Adoptees, I will be breaking away from the past. This series I'll call Recourse and Repatriation, I will touch a little more on Black Elk's vision and segue into a more personal accounting of my own experience of recourse and recovery from RAD. As well as offer my personal understanding of cultural repatriation and spiritual re-acculturation Lakota style.

I am an American Indian, rightly enough. A card carrying one for all it might mean and for whatever purposes to which it matters. And I was adopted at one time. So be it. None of this has ever changed the facts of what really matters. I am a human being and I belong and so do my people. We belong to Mother Earth right here on this the North American continent. Until next time I wish you all enough. Hau Mitakuye Oyasin!

To contact Levi about his workshops for adoptees and repatriation, email him at ironeaglefeather@yahoo.com

*Black Elk Speaks: Being the Life Story of a Holy Man of the Oglala Sioux, October 16, 2008, State University of New York Press; **ISBN-10:** 1438425406.

Please read Levi's essay THE HOLOCAUST SELF in the anthology CALLED HOME: Lost Children of the Indian Adoption Projects, ISBN: 978-0692245880, publisher: Blue Hand Books. www.bluehandbooks.org

9

I'm not alone anymore

Karl Minzenmayer (Ojibwe)

I can usually form intelligible sentences. Evidence suggests otherwise as I keep muttering "Damn, Damn," repeatedly. My eyes can't refrain from staring at John. His piercing blue eyes are mine, his face while stockier is mine too. That jet black hair of his I see every morning in the bathroom mirror. Damn…..

Prior to this moment I was alone in this world. Connected to my Adoptive Parents, wife and son by love and choice. But this is NOT choice. This is the moment that connected me to a full brother I had never met, known of, or dreamed about. In front of me is undeniable physical evidence of a human being I am connected with by BLOOD. I am drowning in the power of my own emotions. Damn…..

I will never be the same.

I was 27 years old that day and John was 23.

I have always known that my sister and I were not related and both adopted. We were given details regarding my Chippewah heritage, my birthmother being only 15 and unable to care for me. To me this meant I was *not* wanted before and my Adoptive Parents *did* want me. No one wondered aloud (near me anyway) why my white parents had these two olive skinned Indian looking kids. Maybe they all knew we were adopted, but I knew I was different.

I felt alone.

As I sit in the Seattle airport across from my brother (who by now is concerned for my vocabulary skills), *I am not alone anymore.*

Karl Minzenmayer was adopted in Washington State by a military family, and has lived in Alaska, Texas, Taiwan, and Colorado. As an adult, Karl found his birth parents and discovered an entire biological family. Being part Ojibwe, he has reconnected with his Native roots. Karl calls Colorado Springs home where he has been a self-employed optician for 29 years. He is a single father of four amazing kids and one great dog. As an Eagle Scout and brother of a special needs sister, Karl is passionate about community service. He is active in non-profit eyewear for kids through the Lions Club and Native Vision, and a volunteer at the Colorado Springs Indian Center. He has been a Camp Counselor and a Special Olympics volunteer. Karl is also an active supporter and member of the National Indian Child Welfare Association (NICWA). This essay was written for Amanda at DeClassified Adoptee blog: http://www.declassifiedadoptee.com

10

Seven Siblings, Two Still Lost

MITZI LIPSCOMB/ROSEMARY BLACKBIRD (Walpole Bkejwanong First Nations)

The restoration of my birth-family has been very good for me in many ways. Not easy, but good nonetheless. I have been able to forge relationships with all my sisters, cousins and my mother. I feel great sorrow for those who have had failed reunions.

I shared about my reunion in the anthology *CALLED HOME: Lost Children of the Indian Adoption Projects* and explained how I was given a copy of a revised birth certificate from the state of Michigan, but I was old enough to remember at the age of 5 that my name had been legally changed at the time of adoption from Rosemary Black-bird to Mitzi Ann Inch.

The trip across the St. Clair River to Ontario's Walpole Island First Nations reserve brought much healing for me as time passed. Often I had felt like "Mork from Ork" in a time when Alex Haleys "Roots" was very much in the news. I was finding my place in my adopted family awkward. There were things that just did not fit. I often felt very much out of place and that my thoughts and feelings were discounted and not of value among the other relatives.

I was blessed with caring and kind christian adopted parents that gave me a good and happy childhood that my birth siblings were not able to have. I lived one block from the elementary school that I attended and had a great group of childhood friends that I am still in contact with. I spent hours playing in the woods, tromping through ponds, camping trips, and enjoying the company of a lovely black Lab that I considered my brother. I was often asked if I had brothers and sisters; I'd reply that I had one brother named "Sam" but not telling them that Sam was a dog.

Mother and Dad never kept anything from me regarding the adoption. For that I am eternally grateful.

Because of that fact I knew that I had siblings somewhere out there. As I went through Port Huron for whatever reason to shop, parades, or the Blue Water Festival, I always had my eyes pealed on every Native face wondering if they were my mother, sister or brother.

I was placed in my last of four foster homes with my adopted Dads sister. She was wonderful! She often rocked me to sleep after I woke from nightmares that plagued me well into my 20's. She saw that my emotional needs were met even though I am sure it interrupted her daily life. I realize now that I had very poor role models in my early years in foster care being moved from one home to another because of physical and sexual abuse.

There was nothing that I wanted more than a brother or sister (or a horse for that matter.) For a period of about a year and a half, an adopted cousin came to live with my family. I was thrilled to have her there and terribly heartbroken that her parents got their lives settled and took her back to live with them. I have to admit that I didn't always treat her as kindly as I should have and regret that to this day. As time went on, I was finding my place in my adopted family awkward. I often felt very much out of place and my thoughts and feelings were discounted and not of value among the other relatives.

Little did I know that during some of my early years, my siblings and birth mother lived three miles away. The farthest that we lived apart was just 70 miles until I graduated from high school; none of my siblings had the opportunity to graduate high school.

My hubby and I were living in Virginia at the time my father and I had a very large blow up about me not being on time to meet he and Mom at a park for a picnic lunch. We were visiting the college that my husband and I attended in Tennessee; my adopted parents agreed to drive from Nashville to meet us halfway from Chattanooga. We were an hour late because of interruptions as we were headed to the car.

Dad was very angry and I knew that he would be. I was anxious as we got closer. I was raised that you were never, never late for any appointment. "It's rude and selfish," I was told after being late for things as a child.

When we arrived at the park Mom and Dad were sitting in the car having waited. I got out of the car to explain and there were a barrage of words exchanged to the point that I told my husband to put both of the boys back in the car and that we were leaving. I felt horrible that I was depriving my kids of the chance to visit with their grandparents they hadn't seen in over six months. At some point I became more rational after seeing tears from my Mom and the kids. So I bit the bullet and said we would stay. It was a very strained short visit.

When we returned to Virginia I was sickened by the event and finally sought out a counselor. During that time I wrote a letter to my Dad apologizing because I felt that if we left the mountain angry with each other and something happened to one or the other, the guilt would be unbearable. For me, it was terrifying that the man that I adored fell from his pedestal. I found that he was capable of failures and imperfections that I had not allowed myself to see.

I worked through the issue with the counselor. On our last visit he commented to me that it might be a good thing if I found my birth family. It would bring some answers to my issues and questions about myself. I had finally vocalized that I trusted very few people in my life, even my husband. I never allowed myself to have any expectations or trust anyone that I meet because I was let down so many times. It was easier to keep a distance than allow myself to be hurt or lose relationships.

The day after the last counseling, my husband and I talked about the visit. He said, "let's start searching again." (Read Called Home for that story.)

A few days later on a Friday night I received a phone call.

"Is this Mitzi?" I stated that it was. She asked me if I had time to sit down and talk. I stepped out the door and sat on the porch of the little house we were living at the time. "OK, I'm sitting down," I replied.

"I'm your oldest sister Bonnie, I remember the day you were taken away." I could feel tears flooding my eyes and gasping for air.

She said, "I cried, My Baby, My baby, why are they taking my baby sister." At that point I lost it with heaving sobs.

After I regained my composure, the questions flew fast and furious. It was wonderful. At last I belonged. I was not an alien dropped from some planet. I had the mother and siblings that I had always looked for all my life. We talked for more than an hour.

The Canadian government had just changed the laws regarding the reinstatement of Indian rights to women that had married non-Indians. Previous to that change, any woman that married a non-Indian was disenfranchised, losing everything with regards to her given rights, including health care, housing, food assistance and treaty settlements. My mother had lost all these because of her marriage to a Caucasian man who worked for a shipping lines that traveled the St. Laurence Seaway.

A day or to later my birth mother called. It was awkward. I first thanked her for not having an abortion for I had now learned that there is no fathers name on my birth certificate. I was too afraid to ask. She went on to tell me how she felt terrible about losing me and my younger siblings to the state. She said that she felt the county Family Services Judge was targeting her and she had no money to hire a lawyer.

It has taken time to build a relationship with Mamma. I send Mother's day cards, and such. We exchange notes and messages through my sister, as Momma is very hard of hearing. I learned she went on to take in a son from one of my cousins that was unable to care for her own son. Mamma raised Johnny as her own. She said it was the least she could do after losing her own children.

Our mother moved around so much to keep ahead of bill collectors and Social Services as she felt that they were after her other children after an accident that resulted in second and third degree burns of my sister Linda. One school year my sisters attended schools in four districts.

About a month after the first phone call my sister Linda Valeri, her husband Bob and three children to visit us for two days, after visiting Bob's Vietnam war buddy in Roanoke, Virginia. It was amazing. We had gestures that were the same. Personal habits that were the same. Identical sense of humor. My husband said it was scary. So much for heredity verses environment!

My middle son Andy said after a recent visit from my sister Linda, "Oh my God, there are two of them?" We burst out laughing and said, "No there are four of us."

As I talked with my Aunties on the rez during my first trip home, I finally figured out that the second call was an Auntie from the other side of the family. When I got off the phone she called my Mamma's sister who happened to be working in the Band office. This is why it took such a short time to find the information that I was looking for. She called my Mamma in the states and gave her my information along with my phone number. This is how my sister Bonnie was able to call the first time.

I was being watched out for as the stars aligned for our reunion.

I am proud to say that I have the siblings that I was always looking for. Seven to be exact.

As the years have passed my sisters often have said that I was the lucky one. I had no idea about the hard times that my sisters had growing up in the Cass Corridor of the ghetto of Detroit. Our mother left the rez and never returned after the death of my brother Anthony who was hit and killed by a drunk driver (who was never prosecuted.) I believe that she was pregnant with me at the time. As time passes, I realize that I would have never survived the things that my sisters lived through. I battled thoughts of suicide in my teens and twenties.

The thirty years that have passed since I first found my birth family, I've spent thousands of dollars in therapy. Sorting out depression and anxiety issues, commitment issues, attachment issues, marriage issues, parenting issues and health issues. Add three years of childhood molestations from a family of boys in elementary school, and a sexual assault while I was in high school. I had a lot to deal with. I now realize that much of these things were a direct result of the crappy first 4 ½ years of my life, leaving me an unwilling victim to the host of problems as I was trying to face life as an adult.

My birth mother is a sweet, feisty, very independent little woman. I now know that she did everything that she could to keep her family together even though she wasn't able. The 1940s, 50s, 60s were terrible times.

Mitzi, right, with her mom and sister

My brother Dale Blackbird is the oldest. He was born with a developmental disability and was taken by the state and placed in an institution for children in Lapeer, Michigan at the age of 7. When the state closed the institution, he was moved to Marysville, Michigan and is living in an adult home.

My oldest sister Bonnie Blackbird-Barrett, who first contacted me, is living just outside of Detroit with her two developmentally disabled sons, and happily retired.

The death of my sister Joanie, Anthony's twin, from cancer pained me very much as I had just begun to get to know her. Her sons and mine resemble each other quite a bit.

My sister Linda Blackbird (Valeri Yanas) is finally remarried to a wonderful man that cares for her in every way. She and I are the closest, as our lives had the most in common. I enjoy hearing from her children. They took the time to work on a relationship each time I came to Michigan to visit.

My story is not complete as I have two younger siblings that were also "stolen" from my mother under false pretenses by the Michigan Department of Social Services.

Lenard Blackbird was born with a clef palate and was sent to foster care until he had surgery to correct his birth defect and then he was adopted. We also have a sister who Mom named Sandra Blackbird who was adopted straight from birth from the Port Huron Hospital.

My adopted mother was present (she was a surgical scrub nurse at the hospital) when both Lenard and Sandra were born via c-section. She contacted social services to see if they were available for adoption. They both were already placed, gone.

We are now searching for both Lenard and Sandra and would love to find and contact them. It is my prayer that sooner or later they, too, will feel "Called Home."

Mitzi contributed an essay SOONER OR LATER, ALL LOST BIRDS COME HOME, in the anthology CALLED HOME: Lost

Children of the Indian Adoption Projects (2014), published by Blue Hand Books.

11

"Oh you were the one who was stolen by the Mormons!"

Leland Kirk Pacheco, Navajo, Maternal clan Many Goats; Kewa (Santo Domingo Pueblo), Turquoise Clan; Pre-I.C.W.A. Adoptee

As an Native Adult Adoptee, certain parts of my history, experiences or what happened before I was adopted change when encountering biological family members and the greeting after I have stated I am Linda Kirk's son is: **"Oh you were the one who was stolen by the Mormons!"**

It is true that I was fostered and adopted into a white Mormon family with nine other adoptees, one which was my biological cousin and seven that were Ojibwe from the Parry Sound Area of Ontario, Canada.

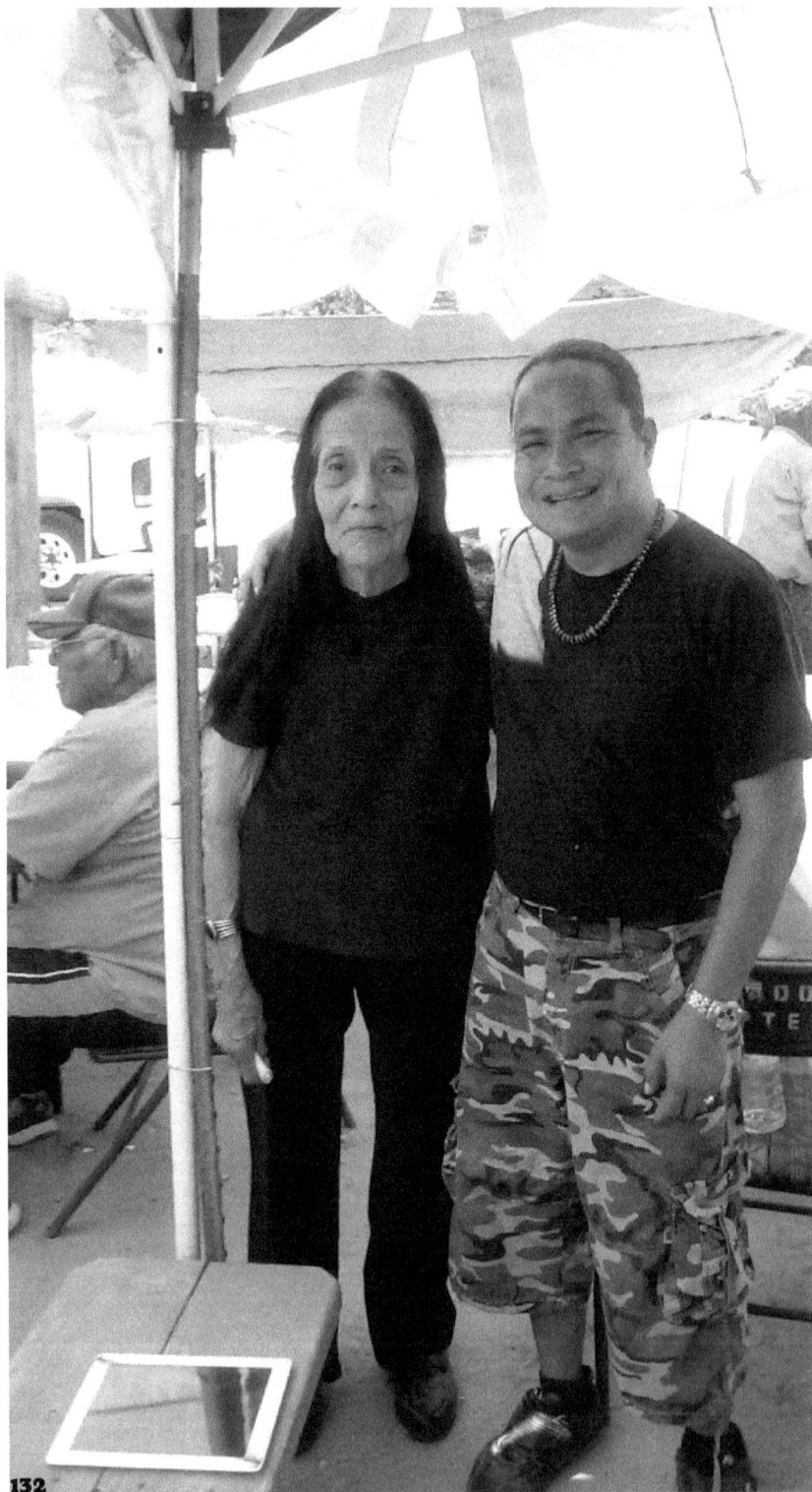

Leland and Grandma Kirk

This year I met my "Grandma" Aunt Ruth Kirk who, back in 1968, took me to the Keams Canyon Indian Hospital for burns on my foot sustained in a fire. She and my "Grandfather" Uncle John Kirk acted responsibly in accessing care, but the fact that the Keams Canyon Hospital found out they were my Grandparents as in the Navajo Traditional Way, at the time, gave the Bureau of Indian Affairs a way to take me from my family, assimilate, foster and adopt out. They started by removing me from the Keams Canyon Hospital and transporting me from Arizona to New Mexico to the Gallup Indian Hospital. This is very clear in my Hospital notes where I was assigned to a caseworker, Mrs. McCray, of Chinle Social Services in Arizona and in the Hospital Records, they had already assigned foster parents.

My maternal family had no idea where I had disappeared to. As my Uncle Ernest told me once, this was during the time of if children lived on the Reservations, if approached by a white person they were told to run! I have been told that time and time again.

This past June 2016 our Kirk Family had the first annual Kirk Family Reunion where hundreds of people showed up during the weekend at my Grandpa Oliver's house. It was so amazing to meet everyone in person after writing to some on Facebook. We keep in touch as much as possible now that we are able to and it sure has been great to meet so many relatives.

It's amazing how ancient our family is. Most live in an area where there are Anasazi ruins and the Petrified Forest. The outlines of the ruins are on the ground. Even though I had been there on one occasion it was unclear that they were there. To look out over a valley from the hilltop where ancient farming took place by the Anasazi and see where the irrigation canals were of their time and to be standing in the same spot where hundreds, if not a thousand years ago, an

Anasazi guard watched over the valley at a lookout, slept in a shelter of several rooms are outlined by their building the base from slabs of petrified tree rock, see the outline of the two kivas of the culture at the time and to view the rock drawings and be told that we are of the Anasazi, the Hopi and the Apache, and we are Diné, Many Goats clan and The Tangled People (clan). It's quite a powerful feeling and suggestion.

As an adoptee we are deprived of this knowledge or history, it is never taught in public schools or universities.

On April 29, 2015 I received a Facebook message from my friend Roxanne who cooked for us at our first annual Native Family Foster Care Recruitment on November 2, 2014 here in Los Angeles:

> "Hello Roxanne.. my name is Marsha and I wondered if u can help my family by getting in contact with Leland Morril. My great uncle Edward from Santo Domingo Pueblo is trying to unite with Leland. My uncle strongly believes Leland is his son and is in search of him. If possible please pass my phone number along to Leland.
> Thank you! 575-xxx-xxxx
> Marsha…"

I was able to talk to my father Edward for the first time on May 1, 2015. We talked for about an hour. It was an amazing conversation I hope every Native adoptee is able to have at some point.

My biological father Edward was at war in 1968 when my mother Linda was killed in a car accident. She had found free day care at St. Anthony's Orphanage for Boys during the day for my little brother Christopher and I while she worked in downtown Albuquerque. So during the weekdays that's where our "daycare" was. It showed how resourceful she was being a first generation Navajo Woman who went out on her own, found a job working for the U.S. Government and provided for us. Also my Aunt Barbara lived with us and did take care of us, as well.

Anyhow, my father did not find out that my mother, the love of his life, had died and that his children were gone: Christopher died of the Hong Kong Flu later that year at the side of Aunt Barbara and in the Navajo Tradition, she prepared the body and buried him in Fort Defiance. Edward's mother (my grandmother) did not think it a good idea to tell him about Linda's passing while he was at war.

After returning back from Vietnam, he did search, and was quite distraught, saddened and depressed, as it was overwhelming.

From our first conversation here are a few words that I recorded:

"I've been trying to ever since I've gotten home from Vietnam and I've been trying to…I was wondering where you were and recently a couple months back somebody told me you were looking for me. I think that was Jimmy."

(Note: I know Jimmy because he comes to Los Angeles for the Autry's Native American Marketplace every fall and I visit with him and his family when they are here.)

"Well, I've been trying to go over to Arizona where they have all those records of the children. And to find if they can locate you but I didn't have any luck in how to get a hold of you. I found out that you were trying to reach me and get a hold of me. I have a lot of information regarding your mom, you know, and I met her over in Haskell, that was really something else."

"Yea Yea, we were both there. We were both there. I met her there. So it was kinda like uh… She was doing a play in the auditorium and I told my friend, I says, I gotta meet that Navajo girl that's up there. He says Yea Yea. I had a chance to meet her on Sunday. The Catholic Church we get together. That's when I met her. We've known each other for a long time. We kinda got together real good you know and over sometimes I see her. But when I was sent to Relocation for a job, the school, was from Haskell we left each other. I didn't see her for a little while.

"She (Linda Kirk) had an accident over in Bernallilo. I don't think you know the place. If you know, right on the freeway. And she was over at the Indian Hospital over in Albuquerque but I was already over in Vietnam when that happened. I couldn't get a hold of her. I can't make any phone calls.

"So, so when she passed away she sent a letter to a friend of mine here in the village (Santo Domingo Pueblo) for me to go down and get you.

"You went to school there but I was already in Vietnam and I didn't know you were placed there because at the time she was, she was in a coma, I understand at the Indian Hospital in Albuquerque and then I guess she knew that she couldn't make it so she sent a letter up here for me to go down to get you but I couldn't get down there, I wasn't home.

"When I came back from Vietnam, my family told me that she had passed away. Because every year she goes her way, we end up back together. We always see each other again regardless of where we go, you know. That year when I came home in '69 when I found out she passed away, I was very hurt. I was hurt that she, she passed on. I think all these years I've been wondering where you were. So I thought you were with your grandfather (Harrison) Mr. Kirk.

"...We talked, we walked in the evenings. It was nice. I looked forward to seeing her every day. Go to breakfast in the morning, lunch and maybe the evening too. We had a lot of good times you know. The only times that were boring with her was during the Christmas vacations she goes home. It was really nice meeting her. I was, I think she was my first love to say, you know?"

So you get the jist of the conversation. It was quite unsettling for me at the time, a lot of information that I had wanted to know but really, it's hard to put your head around a soldier serving at war losing his entire family and coming back to it. Think about a young 20-something soldier with an infant and a toddler and then imagine the horror of his family disappearing and the government he was serving as a soldier taking his surviving child away from him.

My father is an amazing man. He is Santo Domingo Pueblo (Kewa) and lives in the traditional way.

Leland and cousins

I was able to meet him and some of my cousins and his sister, my Aunt Jesse and in August 2015 during the annual Feast Day Celebration at the Santo Domingo Pueblo.

Not only that, another shocker to me was during the dancing in the Plaza, everyone had my body type. I was in complete awe of how beautiful that was to watch and to see another part of my biological connection as they danced in the plaza. My cousin Marlene let me stay at her home in Albuquerque and I am grateful to her for that.

On the subject of activism and keeping the momentum up for Native Adoptees, I attended two NICWA Conferences, National Indian Child Welfare Association. In 2014 I was a presenter as a Pre-ICWA Adoptee, and in 2015 I was an attendee. At the end of the 2015 NICWA Conference in Portland I provided testimony at the Bureau of Indian Affairs proposed "*Regulations for State Courts and Agencies in Indian Child Custody Proceedings.*"

Here in Los Angeles I have been a "regular" at our local ICWA Taskforce. We've had two annual Native Foster Parent Recruitment events, on November 2, 2014 and September 26, 2015. I have spoken at both recruitment events. Many people plan these events and it does take a fair amount of effort and time. Our ICWA Task Force and the American Indian Unit of the Los Angeles County Department of Children and Family Services both planned these. They were well-attended. We had the Navajo Times run an article for the 2014 event and FNX (First Nations Xperience) public television station here in San Bernardino ran ads for both events.

"Date: Mon, Oct 13, 2014 at 10:46 AM
Subject: Re: ICWA Task Force awareness request for Los Angeles County Native American Foster Families event.
To: Lee Morrill
Good morning Leland,
The CEO/Publisher has decided to proceed with publishing your event in the PSA section. The info will publish up to the date of the event.
Vernon Yazzie, Advertising/Sales Manager, Navajo Times Publishing Company, Inc.

I was also able to travel June 2015 to be a keynote speaker at the Montana Tribal Social Services Association Conference and talk about being a Pre-ICWA Native Adoptee and to share information and insight there with their tribal communities.

I will close with a small personal highlight. A project that came out this was aired on *Comedy Central* this passed November on Drunk History's "POPE LEADS THE PUEBLO REVOLT" Season 3, Episode 10. They used many of the Natives to play background characters. I did find out later while talking to some other Santo Domingo Pueblo people that this was for the Northern Pueblo Nations.

I learned that there were two revolts. The second is not written but an oral history.

http://www.cc.com/video-clips/32ri3c/drunk-history-pope-leads-the-pueblo-revolt"

As you can see so much for the positive has happened with my life beyond the search. I would encourage those adoptees who have the courage and the ability to reach out to their local native communities and become involved. You will be surprised how many Natives are adoptees or foster children or had some sort of removal story. Being able to be part of the process is extremely healing.

Thanks for reading all the narratives in this book. Mine is but one of hundreds of thousands. Remember approximately 30% of Native children of my generation were removed through foster care and adoption.

Leland contributed his reunion story in TWO WORLDS and CALLED HOME.

12

My Misun

Dana Lone Hill (Oglala Lakota)

The following story I wrote for *Last Real Indians* after I searched for and found my brother. Never give up on our relatives.

I decided to write this strictly from my heart. Without interviewing anyone, without researching facts or stats and without the aid of the ever glorious Google and Wikipedia.

I am writing this with the hand of cards I was dealt with in life and the role I now treasure.

As a big sister.

If anyone out there is the oldest daughter or son of one or more younger siblings, you know it is kind of a pain in the ass, right?

You are an expert at changing diapers, making bottles, and can calm a crying baby even before you ever think to have your own. Your one hip automatically juts out in that way of carrying chubby babies around even before they become child bearing hips. In fact, more than once your swear, you won't have kids yourself.

I, however did have kids. Two in a row when I was 20 and 21. And my mom was still having kids, also. So our kids grew up together. Do you think having my own kids relieved me of some sisterly duties? Well, it would have because my mom moved to Minnesota, but I followed her and had twice as many dirty diapers to change. It was challenging, but I guess looking back, I was in my prime of life. A young mother and a big sister at the same time, not even knowing I was doing amazing things that would put your average stay at home suburban mother on valium and make her rack up a huge psychiatrist bill because this isn't what life was supposed to be about in her daydreams.

And to me, it wasn't what life was supposed to be. I was supposed to move to New York, become a writer of awesome books, and spend summer days with the Bombers in the Bronx. But as life had it, I became a mother and a big sister.

The first time and only time I recall seeing my little brother Wakiya, he was four years old and he had long, shiny braids. He was in a grocery store with his mom and my mom pointed with her lips, "Look, that's your little brother, go say hi."

I walked over, said hi to his mom. I remembered her from her relationship with my dad. Then I looked at my little brother. He had huge eyes. In fact he looked like my brother Travis, but with long hair. He looked at me and smiled one of the largest smiles I ever saw. I remember knowing in my heart he was my little brother. I gave him an awkward hug and walked away. I was maybe 14 or 15. And that was the last time I saw him.

Years later, in my 20s I had heard he was lost in the foster care system. My heart broke a little but I hoped it wasn't true.

Wakiya was always in my heart though. I would do something in life and realize how wonderful life is. Even when it was something small like decorating a Christmas tree with an ornament one of my kids made and my heart would tug at me. As if it was reminding me and telling my subconscious, Did your little brother make an ornament for someone's tree? Did they use it? Do they appreciate what he can do?

I would wonder when I saw reunion editions of talk shows like Oprah on TV and think "Man, I wished I could get Oprah's attention and tell her I have a little brother out there."

I did a speech in a class I took at the College of St. Catherine, it was a collage of sorts about what is important in your life. I knew I was going to cry, partly in fear of public speaking and partly because if my speech. I made a spinning dreamcatcher. I shaped it so it would spin because I felt like that is how life was, in constant motion. I wove different color and shaped rocks in it. The rocks represented my anchors and purpose in life, my children. A feather hanging from the center represented my path in my life. Which, at the time I had thought was centered. Certain beads represented my family members and then there was a little feather on its own. Off to the side, but connected. That was my brother Wakiya. Why, my instructor asked, was he not a bead? Because I don't know where he is! – I sobbed.

Many times I told myself no, I can't find him because this is not how life works out. I am not one of those people that can make magic things like that happen. I am not hand picked by Oprah. I realize now I told myself this was impossible before I even tried or realized that anything in life is possible. I even tried learning sign language because I had heard this was how he communicated. Plus, I also think it is an amazing, beautiful language and am proud one of my sons wants to major in this field. Anyway this rumor proved to not be true, he can talk and he can talk and he can talk.

When The Guardian out of the United Kingdom decided to let me keep writing after my Thanksgiving story, I talked to my mom about important issues I had thought needed to be addressed in Indian Country. We knew, especially after the *NPR report* of how South Dakota was using the foster care system to remove Indian children from their homes and place them in homes of non-natives as a sort of cash cow. Not only do foster homes receive money for each child, they also receive extra for Native children because South Dakota will classify every Native child in any system as "special needs" whether they are special needs or not, so top dollar will be received. This would be why some families only take in Native children. The big misconception of young Indian mothers or families is to assume that their children are better off in foster homes and assume that everyone getting a fat paycheck for the *Wakanyeja* (God's Sacred Gift) are in it because they have a big heart. I believe some people do have good hearts, but not everyone on the native child foster care payroll does, which is what always worried me.

And that is why I wanted to write about my brother. I started looking at life with a different attitude last year and realizing anything was possible. Telling myself I have the power in me to make things happen. I didn't go about looking for my brother the way the state told me to, which would immediately discourage anyone. I don't hold a grudge at them for not contacting me when I was 19 to keep him, and I didn't listen to reason. Instead, I found out his name. And I googled him.

I googled him every day, sometimes looking up to hit the F5 button until I started getting hits. They came in, like a timeline. Starting with him being in the obituary section of losing an adopted sibling here and there.

To him winning art contests, races, etc. And then I got the hit that included a picture. My brother is an awesome Special Olympics champion in relays and races. And I found a newsletter with pictures. And I found a picture of him..

My heart stopped, I cried. It was two years old but got dammit I was going to write the number and email down.

It was a group home in Texas. It took me three weeks to get the courage to call because the email I sent with a link to my Guardian story about him was never answered. Finally I put my "phone voice" on, which is official as hell (no rez slang), and called. I was transferred to my brothers case worker and I was prepared to fight the best way I know how, with words. I wasn't sure of laws, if I was in the wrong, or anything – but I was prepared to let them know this was my little brother and I loved him. I was prepared for the snotty attitude I'm used to from most social workers, etc.

Instead I got John Wayne, or someone who sounded just like John Wayne. I discovered my brother's caseworker was a wonderful man, with a Texas drawl who easily could be telling you to "saddle up pardna." I explained my story, my unanswered email, and told him Wakiya was the missing piece in my heart.

He didn't have attitude, he didn't disbelieve me, which is the norm for most caseworkers here in South Dakota, instead he told me, give me a few minutes and Wakiya and I will call you back.

The first time I talked to Wakiya, we jammed his caseworkers phone and we cried for over an hour. "God bless you sister, I have been praying for this day," he said. I told him what his name means, why it is important in our family and how I needed him. He cried and said, "I knew in my heart I would be found."

So now he is back. He made his own choice to come back to the state that somehow made the decision that a family in Texas could raise him better than any of his real family. And at age 29, he was on his own. **They gave up on him and he had no contact with the family who adopted him.** Not that it bothered him to be afloat in the state of Texas. If I learned one thing about my brother and from my brother, no matter what cards life dealt him, he is resilient. He moves on with the biggest smile in the world.

How can I even describe these feelings I feel since he is back?

It is unreal. He is home. Life goes by in a flashes and in flashes, I learned to never take a moment for granted, don't let what others do make you miserable, let go of the negative and accept happiness. Meeting my brother was a moment in my life of complete joy and pure 100% happiness. There have been few moments in my life of that kind of happiness: playing in the leaves with my dad and little brother, sleeping with my great grandma and grandpa, hearing my Grandpa Rusty sing while he cooked, being around family at kettle dance and hearing the songs, the birth of all four children, hearing my kids laugh, knowing the feel of freedom, watching as my sons graduated, and now meeting the brother that was missing all my life, ranks up there with a moment in my life of pure 100% happiness.

Wakiya is only a success story of the foster care system because he is resilient, like our ancestors. The hurt, pain, rejection, and loneliness he felt and with what he went through would take down the strongest of hearts and largest of spirits. And both sides of his family are overwhelmed with his presence. He is changing lives with just being here, his mom said. He sure is. He is magical like that, that little brother of mine.

My *misun*. (Little brother.)

Indian people, do not let our children go. Do not assume because a state run facility chooses who raises them means they are people with bleeding hearts, full of compassion and want to raise our beautiful, brown children out of the goodness of their hearts.

Remember we all have rights, there is still a fight in each of our spirits, and don't let the government get you down.

After all, anything is possible. Like finding a long lost brother after 20 plus years, and I didn't even need Oprah.

Welcome home, Misun. Like he said that day in the park as we listened to a horrible cover of Bob Marley's Three Little Birds. "The past is the past, but we are here now."

Nothing but love.

Wakiya and Dana

Dana Lone Hill is the author of *Pointing With Lips: A Week in The Life of a Rez Chick*, published in 2014 by Blue Hand Books. www.bluehandbooks.org

13

The Fence

Joseph M. Pierce (Cherokee)

The leather gloves are starting to blister my fingers. It is summertime in South Texas, and we're building a fence. I am 13 years old.

My parents have just purchased a 10-acre plot after several years of renting both a house and a separate barn to keep our horses. My younger brother and I have been enlisted to help build this fence so that we can finally bring the horses to our new home. On one half of the property the earth is sandy, easy to work with; on the other, closer to the brackish bay at the end of our land, it is hardened clay, impenetrable, insufferable.

How do you learn to build a fence? How do your hands learn to twist those ties, to drive the tamp, to force the auger slowly, stubbornly, down into the earth?

I still have a scar on my left hand from when I got a finger stuck in that auger.

I am thinking about fences for two reasons. The first has to do with my relationship with my father. The second has to do with a man named John Rock. He is our Cherokee ancestor, born in 1855, and listed on the Dawes Rolls. He is the genealogical starting point that connects us to that moment and that history.

When I think about my relationship with adoption, however, I have to clarify (and this is important) that it was my father who was adopted, not me. Even if I look very little like my mother, and have often been asked if I am, in fact adopted. I was not. But my father was. And by a loving white family, who brought him to Kilgore, Texas, in the early 1950s.

Still, I want to think about what type of relationship I can have, I do have, with adoption and with the Cherokee Nation. And I want to think about this in terms of bodies and the law.[*]

It isn't clear why my father was put up for adoption, but we can try to understand the circumstances. It was 1952 and his mother was Native, his father was white, and they weren't married. He was delivered in San Antonio, Texas, and a Baptist adoption agency connected his mother with a white family that wanted to adopt a child. By all accounts, it was a successful adoption. By this I mean that my father had a life that he probably would not have had as the mixed-race child of an unwed, 20-year-old mother in rural Oklahoma. My father grew up in a supportive environment, went to college, read books, got a good job, met my mother, got married, had kids. He is a good man, a generous man, and I admire this in him.

He doesn't talk about being adopted, though. He doesn't talk about that part of his background, even if now we have connected with his Cherokee family, our Cherokee family, who we finally met in 2006. My father was 54 when he first met his mother, Ada. She came to the meeting with her daughter from a subsequent marriage, Lori, who said that they always knew my father existed, but didn't have any way of contacting him, of doing anything about it. Ada would also say during that meeting that she was so worried that my father, her son, would think ill of her. Her face was so vulnerable in that moment. It made me wonder: What trace does his birth leave behind?

We all spent time together in Oklahoma on a few occasions after that initial meeting, and went through the process of becoming citizens of the Cherokee Nation. When Ada was diagnosed with cancer, yet again, my father was able to drive up to see her, to make peace with her before she passed in 2014.

Ada was 20 when my father was born. She was working at a diner in the Oklahoma panhandle. She would have been entirely unable to care for him on her own. And she decided, she was able to decide, that giving him up for adoption would have been the best for him. It was, in this sense a sacrifice that she made conscientiously. This is not one of those egregious cases of Native adoption in which she was coerced, or forced, to give him away. Unless we consider the history of Native displacement, of settler colonialism, the sinister continuation of Native marginalization, of theft.

But it is no less important, in my opinion, to think about what that adoption means in time and in bodies. As embodied. I mean that we all have histories, we adoptees or children of adoptees, have histories that we don't know, that we can't know, that we don't have access to. That inaccessibility is part of what makes the process so vexing. It is not that my father blames Ada, he doesn't. But there is a wound, psychic or otherwise, that develops around the issue. And that is not easy to figure out, to come to terms with, to deal with. What cauterizes this wound?

The embodiment of this process is what I am trying to describe. That is what I am recalling with the opening scene of my father, brother, and me building a fence. Because it was perhaps another fence that illustrates this embodiment. It is the fence that John Rock had to build around the land that he was allotted in the 19th century.

Ironically, (how could these events be connected?) only three months after my father's birth, a law suit was brought against the heirs of John Rock: "Take notice that you have been sued in the District Court of McIntosh County, Oklahoma by W. R. Williams and Mary V. Williams, as Plaintiffs, and you must answer Plaintiff's petition on or before the 25th day of April 1952, or judgment will be entered quieting the title of plaintiffs to the lands".

It is stunning to think of what this implies. I don't have the backstory, but the original allotment of John Rock, and, I imagine, the fence that he would have had to build around his land, was being contested in court in McIntosh County. What for? What was the outcome? I don't know. But it is telling that the land that was once his, John's, five generations removed from my father, who had just been born and given up for adoption, was under suit. The land that was allotted to him after the forced removal was about to be taken away.

But I wonder, too, what would John Rock's fence have looked like. What would the scene of his building that fence have included? Did he also enlist his sons to help him build it? Did he have a fence at all? Did his hands have scars like mine?

Psychology might refer to these questions under the rubric of genetic memory. In dance, it might suggest what Martha Graham called "blood memory." But I do not want to delve too deeply into theoretical discussions here. I do, however, want to imagine the act of building a fence in terms of what it might mean for connecting to an unreachable but imaginable past. This is the past that could not have existed for the adoptee, these are the stories, those are the scars, the movements, the gestures, that were once part of the family tradition, and which are foreclosed by adoption.

But building a fence is not complicated. It depends on a few standard, if variable practices. Movements that while certainly marked by time and technology, by culture, and by necessity, are also movements that share a certain kinetic affinity. What might it have meant to build that fence, our fence, in the same way as John Rock did 100 years earlier? What might our movements have had in common? Or what did they, without us knowing?

On the other hand, it might be a strange object to dwell on, a fence, when talking about the relationship between indigeneity and adoption. A fence is often imagined as a barrier, to demarcate space, to keep intruders out, to protect the family within. But I want to think, too, of the fence as a site of embodied practice, a place where the hands that twist ties and tamp posts might share a sense of history.

Even if my father rarely talks about his adoption, when we were finally able to open the sealed adoption records, to make contact with that family, and to meet in person, there was no animosity. If anything I remember that scene as measured and somewhat melancholic. Our voices were slow and tentative, our faces scanning, searching for a gesture, a look that might connect us. Faces yearning for recognition and, perhaps, forgiveness.

But there was nothing to forgive. "We always knew you existed," as my new aunt said. And I think that is something that we have to keep in mind when we try to work through the scenes of Native adoption and reconciliation. "We always knew you existed" is a phrase that marks the position of the adoptee both in the past and in the present; it is an arc of relation that is continuous. My father was not forgotten. Quite the opposite. His presence was always there, his body perhaps absent, but the memory of that presence, or the imagination of what and where his body might be, continued, if even spectrally—hauntingly—, from the day of his birth to the moment we were reunited.

That animates my thinking about John Rock and his fence, about what the work of memory and of gesture has to do with dealing with the present of an adoptee. What memory can my father have of the past that he was never meant to have? Or, alternatively, what memory can we construct, assemble, out of the fragments of history that we begin to comprehend only later?

Perhaps the fence, in this sense, becomes the metaphor that I am looking for. It is as a collective effort of tying and braiding, of staking out, and stretching material across time and space, that might actually be the psychic and embodied process that animates adoptees in history. To build this fence is not to keep someone out, it is to work together toward a common goal, toward resolution, toward kinship. To work toward kinship, in this sense, is to take stock of the relations we embody and which are also marked by history, histories we know and which we don't know, and by time and materials. To work toward kinship is not to become something you are not. It is to feel the movement, the weight, of time and body, to build, to structure, to embody the relations that you might never have known, but always knew were there.

*I have written about this elsewhere, in an essay republished in Indian Country Today as, "In Search of an Authentic Indian: Notes on the Self," http://indiancountrytodaymedianetwork.com/2015/07/28/search-authentic-indian-notes-self-161129

Joseph M. Pierce is Assistant Professor in the Department of Hispanic Languages and Literature at Stony Brook University. His research focuses on kinship, gender, and sexuality in Latin America and on hemispheric discourses of citizenship and belonging. He is a citizen of the Cherokee Nation. His website: www.josephmpierce.com

14

Dreaming in Indian

Mary St. Martin (Koyukon Athabascan)

I've always dreamt in Indian. Vivid, lucid, in color and shaded with symbols. One evening night quest, my body was carried in a stream. The water above and below me flowed horizontally from my head toward my toes. However, my body was carried in a current of its own and moving me ahead. As I approached a steep hill, I began to struggle. My brief panic subsided when I chose not to lose my strength fighting the elements I could not control. I reached deep in cool water with both hands. Waiting below were fish who sucked on my fingers and pulled me the rest of the way home. I think I am a Salmon. Instinctively, I was called home.

In the year of 2014 I located my cousins and my Koyukon Athabascan tribe. I was welcomed with tears. Even first cousin Barb felt like she needed to have a baby shower. When my tax return came in February 2015, the first thing I did was make reservations from Los Angeles to Fairbanks, Alaska and second reservation with a bush plane to fly me to the Village of Koyukuk. The Native Village of Koyukuk lies where the Koyukuk river meets the Yukon. About 300 miles from Fairbanks. No running water to the cabins. No roads in and out.

I landed in Fairbanks at 12 a.m. The summer sun still shown during mid-July midnight. I was met with an aunt and several cousins. As I came down the escalator from the terminal, I was welcomed with Athabascan singing, tears and hugs. My first cousin LaVern opened her house to me and organized a family reunion for the next evening; Barb took the day off work to spend with me. I had my first ever family reunion with people related to me, my first native food and first stories of my father's life.

A day later LaVerne flew with me into Koyukuk, where my father lived and died on the river. I cannot begin to explain my emotions at this time. I cried real tears. Tears I could not control. I had emotions and questions overcoming my sense of self. Anxiety set in. I began to ask myself... am I crazy? What the hell am I doing flying over 2k miles and into the interior of Alaska on a bush plane to meet people and see a way of life that my DNA says I am half of? I am nuts?

I was crying inside the plane before I even exited. My heart beating fast and I could feel it. I could see my first cousin Marylin. I could see Marilyn was just as scared as I was. I could see people arriving to meet the plane on their quads and in trucks. Even the unleashed dogs came to welcome.

Lump in my throat, crying and shaking I got out of the plane. I embraced Marilyn first. Then the rest of the group. One by one they hugged me, introduced themselves and welcomed me "home."

They held a huge banner which read "Welcome" and once again I was serenaded with beautiful voices singing in Athabascan.

The next few days were life-changing for me. Another reunion dinner was held. I ate more Native food including moose, beaver, salmon and muktuk (whale blubber). After dinner an Elder presented me with an Indian name that Marilyn chose for me. I still could not believe my ears when people welcomed me "home."

During my stay, I got to see cousins LaVern and Peter catch Salmon on the Yukon. While seining, I was reminded of my dream. I thank the spirit of the Salmon for guiding me home and providing food for our people. I want to go back home now even stronger than before.

I know now first-hand what I am missing and what has been imprinted in me for many generations. My DNA...my endless imprint from past, present to future which still calls me home.

It is this present generation of Native adoptees who need to continue to find our way home. It is you, it is me. We must follow our instinct and swim upstream. Some of us make it, some won't but you still need to keep swimming. If you don't fight back, the predators win. It's in our DNA and a matter of survival for Natives today and future generations. Trust the forces that pull you through to carry us home. Keep swimming upstream for yourself and all adoptees.

15

Singing the Moon

Patricia Busbee (Cherokee)

Young Patricia

I recently returned to the Pacific Northwest after living in Asheville, N.C. for the last four years. I am in the same town, Olympia, Washington, that I was living in when I learned of my Native ancestry. Prior to moving to North Carolina I attended Evergreen State College and Goddard College. (Both of these colleges have been heavy on my mind and until this morning I had no idea why. As I wrote this update I had a realization regarding my life journey and my writing career).

The majority of my professors at Evergreen were Native American. At that time I had no idea of my ancestry. I just knew I was drawn there. I loved the Longhouse. One of the professors, Gail

Tremblay, wrote the letter that opened the door for me to go to grad school. She is Mi'kmaq–Onondaga. She is an amazing artist that works in many mediums. She weaves baskets out of old film. I was sitting next to her when she typed my letter to Goddard. Since I had no clue about my father's ancestry, I never imagined in my wildest fantasies that after graduation I would be writing about my own ancestry. It just wasn't part of my reality—and yet it was.

What I missed is the connection between my acceptance into Goddard and what took place at my graduation—the exiting process. A few days before I graduated all the adoption documents I uncovered were confirmed. I was in shock. A few hours before walking down the aisle to receive my diploma I told my story to a Native author at Goddard. She was very gracious and supportive. I was barely holding myself together. She provided me with resources. She was my link to Trace/Lara.

My entire writing career and my education is rooted in the support of Native artists, educators and professors. How could I not see this in its entirety? I must have had on blinders made of steel. Whenever I vacillate and think that maybe I should be writing mainstream fiction or something more lucrative—please, somebody, call me out.

What I am sure about is the healing power of words and stories. This is where I want to focus my time and energy. This is the path I want to follow. I am not entirely sure of what that looks like yet but I am very close.

Coming back, coming full circle to where this journey began has been very powerful. I am ready to excavate more pieces of my adoption story. There are still loose ends. I take sabbaticals to stay sane. Currently I am on a mission to locate a picture of my biological grandmother.

I have spent a lot of time being angry over my adoption, over the lies, the tales and fabrications that were told to me. And rightly so.

But if I pull the curtain back just a little I can also see that I did not make this journey alone.

The four years I spent in North Carolina were very healing. I connected with a teacher on the Qualla Boundary. I have been studying with him for eighteen months. He is a therapist and works with the school system on the reservation. He is in his seventies. He is also of mixed ancestry. His mother was Cherokee. He grew up both on and off the reservation. He taught me how to pay attention to nature and the signs around me. He also taught me about Cherokee history. Most of our interactions were focused on integrating the wounded aspects of myself.

I mentioned in my other pieces that I am a spiritual person. It troubled me that I had no clue how to pray or how to practice. That has changed since having a teacher. I may not have a lot of knowledge about how my ancestors practiced/worshipped but I learned I can connect with Great Spirit thru prayer, honoring the earth, educating myself, giving back, making myself useful and thru trusting and understanding that I have made it this far.

After lots of back and forth I let go of my Hindu/Eastern studies and practices. I let go of most of my prior spiritual practices in order to embrace and walk the path of my Ancestors—even though I do not fully understand what that means. It's all right that I do not have a manual or a book that tells me how to do it. So far my ancestors have done a pretty good job of opening doors and connecting me to the people I need to have in my life.

It's interesting to find myself back in the Seattle area but from a very different perspective and with a lot of miles behind me. I guess I had to walk in several other worlds first. And I needed to explore and ponder my educational process as I transition into the next stage of my writing career. I can't hide and vacillate any longer and wonder what it is I should be writing about. If I continued in that in-between space, I think my ancestors would have wacked me over the head with a frying pan.

Along with reuniting the past with the present there have been a few other major highlights.

1) I had coffee with two of my brothers on my father's side. I visited them at their homes. Both lost their wives due to illness last year. One struggles terribly with me and the other embraces me. The one that struggles has issues with understanding that his father, my father, was in his forties during my conception and my mother was sixteen. He called my mother a "Run Around." I almost got up and left but he clearly was hurting. I am glad the door between us remains open.

2) My sister Beth and I went to our mother's, grandmother's and my father's grave. All reside in the same cemetery. Most of the graveyard was a swamp due to the heavy rains. We were ankle deep in water. We said prayers spoken from the heart and left offerings of food and alcohol. Beth remembers our mother. I have no memory of her. Beth still has no leads regarding her father.

3) I returned to my childhood town and to the house I grew up in. I am still processing the flood of memories that came forward as soon as I turned onto my street. I experienced it like an emotional drive-by. The oak saplings had grown into tall stately trees. Several neighbors watched as I took pictures of my childhood home. My adoptive father's rosebushes had long since vacated the property. I wanted to sit down on the front steps and sort out my emotions—pick thru them like piles of laundry.

4) I attended a family reunion and met an uncle I had no idea even existed. He was my mother's half brother. He was kind and helpful. He was able to provide insight into my mother thru the stories he told. This was especially helpful as a lot of what I have is documents. It is the stories I crave.

5) I met the woman that provided me with my first documents regarding my ancestry. I cried the moment I saw her.

6) I spent an extended amount of time with a nephew that is also an adoptee. It was very healing.

7) Since I returned to the Seattle area I have been asked to take part in a monthly women's sweat for healing. Tribal elders lead it. This is within the Veteran's community. My husband is a Vietnam veteran that suffers from PTSD. I am very excited to connect with this group.

8) I reunited with my granddaughter. This is very powerful and a huge healing for my entire family—especially my daughter. My daughter and her daughter were separated for several years. Reunification was the motivating factor as to why we moved across country. I am hoping that somehow this heals our matriarchal line. I once had someone tell me that my matriarchal line was cursed. Someone else said our karma was corrupted. I have no idea if any of this is true but I do know that a large majority of the women in my family have lost their children due to adoption, death, imprisonment, alcohol, drug abuse, mental illness and rape. No more! May the women in my bloodline heal.

I am aware that my emotional landscape surrounding adoption can shift like the weather. Today I feel strong. Tomorrow I may not be able to keep my sadness at bay. I have come to understand that untangling my history has been powerful, healing, horrifying and life altering. The process changed me in ways I never imagined.

Patricia Busbee's website: www.singingthemoon.me

Patricia is the author of *Remedies*, published by Blue Hand Books in 2012, www.bluehandbooks.org. She was co-editor and contributor of *Two Worlds* and *Called Home: Lost Children of the Indian Adoption Projects. (see biblio in this book)*

16

Aftermath

Susan Devan Harness (Confederated Salish Kootenai Tribes)

Prior to 2013 I was considered, by some, to be an anti-adoption activist, specifically with regard to American Indian child adoption. And there was good reason: I wrote fiercely about adoption as an aspect of historic trauma. I vehemently questioned the moral role of legislation in determining and defining the legitimacy of a family, a person, a representative of an ethnic group. Adoptions were bad; staying within family/community was good. As I saw it, there was no middle ground.

My world, that year, would be shaken to the core and turned upside down. It's difficult, then, to hold fast to your perspective. In fact, I couldn't. I had no other choice, but to embrace my new reality.

It's all about survival.

***

The Flathead Indian reservation was a place I'd wanted to call home for most of my life. And in a way, it was. I am a tribal member; I spent the first eighteen months living with my birth family, before being adopted by a white couple. I spent most of my life trying to return. So for the month of June that year, that is where I went to write my memoir.

A friend lent me her condo, one that sat a mere fifty feet from the shores of Flathead Lake, and I sat in the kitchen or the living room and wrote, sometimes for eleven hours a day. Breaks gave me time to visit brothers and sisters, aunts and uncles, cousins and friends. Most of my time was spent with my sister, Ronni, who introduced me to the land and the people as much as she could. This place, these visits, informed me about my family, thereby informing me about my removal.

Many adoptees dream of *going home* and some write of that homecoming as healing. For me it wasn't healing; it was destabilizing. It forced me to discard my rose-colored glasses and see my birth-family and the community in which they lived as they existed, not as I wanted them to be. In doing so, I had to face a couple of very important truths that are entirely side-stepped in the adoption debate: sometimes there are very good reasons children are removed from their families. And sometimes there are very good reasons they cannot be placed with extended family. The former I'll get to in a few moments; the latter was purely economics. My grandparents, as well as aunts and uncles, were already caring for several of their grandchildren, or their nieces and nephews; they were not able to take in three more, my sister and brother and me. Not on their limited incomes and resources.

***

My adoption, and the reasons for it, were quickly shunted aside when Riley our grandson born the November the previous year, began vomiting blood in early September. He was airlifted to Children's Hospital Colorado, where he was met on the tarmac by the liver-team and rushed to the Pediatric Intensive Care Unit, where we all waiting for a pediatric liver. Day after day I walked by glass doors, whose rooms contained children fighting for their lives, while adults stood helplessly by. On December 13, 2013, we were one of those adults; Riley had lost the fight. The pediatric liver never arrived.

***

My world, once strong and unbending, became liquid with my cancer diagnoses. Three weeks before Riley's death I'd been diagnosed with breast cancer. Three weeks after I'd been diagnosed with uterine cancer. I stopped asking what more could happen next. I didn't want to know. January was surgeries, February the start of chemo, June the beginning of the daily radiation treatments that would last for two months. It was in the midst of these treatments that I lost my mom, the woman who'd adopted me.

Mom was my rock. She gave me love, guidance and safety. She taught me everything she felt it was important for me to know. There was the home stuff, the cooking, sewing, the canning. But there was the life stuff. Like how to make guests feel welcome: "You always offer a guest something to eat and drink before you do anything else." The value of education: "That's the one thing no one can ever take away from you." And the appreciation of every day: she'd point out bluebells, exclaim over the explosive yellows and purples of pansies, or stare in awe at the brilliant color of sunsets. And when I got older, she also framed the idea of power and sealed records, specifically my adoption records: "No one should know anything about you that you don't know about yourself."

What she didn't teach me, perhaps couldn't teach me, was how to have difficult conversations. So we didn't talk about my cancer. That was too frightening. It was difficult enough talking with her ten years previous about my research for my cultural anthropology thesis. That was one of the memories that lay heavy on me as I sat on the edge of her bed and held her hand over the last three days of her life.

For two years I'd been able to side-step the topic. She knew I was taking classes, but I didn't tell her what they were about, or why I was doing them. She didn't know about the tears as I sat in my advisor's office and related the stories of Native adoptees that came out in my interviews. She didn't know the havoc they wreaked within my spirit. But as my defense day loomed closer, a mere two weeks away, I wanted her there. I felt she deserved to be there.

So I issued the invitation while I was driving us to lunch.

"What is your research about?" she asked after I broached the topic. "I don't think you've ever told me." Ten years later I can still recall exactly where we were at that moment: driving down College Avenue. It was early April and the grass was brilliant green and the buds on the trees lining the street were swollen with the promise of spring.

I explained about historic trauma, the Indian Adoption Project and its role in legislating child placement for Indian kids. As I talked I became aware of her silence. It wasn't an angry silence, it was a quiet silence. But it was uncomfortable and heavy, too laden with possibilities for misinterpretation. I blurted, "It isn't about you, Mom. It's about me, what it was like to be me trying to live in this place surrounded by so many people who looked so different than me, and had expectations as to what I should be, and how I should act. It's not about you. You're the best mom I could have ever asked for."

Silence continued to fill that small car. It stopped the air from moving, it stopped my ability to think, to breathe. It stopped time. It was finally broken by mom's trembling voice asking, "You mean you came available because of a government program? That I took you away from your family?"

Pain wrapped in confusion.

My words were out and I couldn't take them back. Ever.

Two weeks later, Mom sat at my defense and listened to my argument that the Indian Adoption Project being a continuation of various and sundry assimilation programs. It was, I'd stated, the most tragically successful assimilation program to date. I watched her as she nodded, and smiled. She congratulated me, and she accepted congratulations from my professors for raising a strong daughter. I saw then, that her love had no boundaries. Even though it hurt, she supported my activism.

★★★

I look back now and my experiences as a child, a sister, a mother and an aunt have all been tinged by adoption. With every turn of the kaleidoscope, colors and textures and patterns burst and reform anew, so much so that I no longer know what that original pattern was supposed to be. All I know is there is a certain guilt that goes with my experiences as an adoptee.

And when the guilt is associated with my mom, through no fault of her own, I want so badly to take back the anguish that was caused by this outside *thing*, this event that has been forced on us, that has to be accepted by us, but without a rule book as to how to go about doing that acceptance.

***

After Riley died and Mom died, and after the completion of my cancer treatments and Rick's cancer treatments—he'd been diagnosed two years before—, after the first wave of grief (but certainly not the last) had passed I paused for just a moment. In that pause I felt the fabric of my existence rip, destroying the narrow kaleidoscope that had informed my life.

I was born in 1959, long before the Indian Child Welfare Act of 1978 had been legislated. Its purpose was assimilation. I was never supposed to find my way home. My adoptive parents were never supposed to allow me to 'be' Indian. I was supposed to be 'one of us', with full and complete access to the American Dream. Except it didn't really work out that way.

Yes, I paid a social price for being Indian, and yes, I paid a social price for acting white; yes, I wished that I'd been allowed to know my birth-family; yes, for too many years I had no idea who I was or who I was supposed to be; and, yes, I resented the social Durkheimian 'facts' that were being forced on me, ascribing my characteristics, my behaviors, my way of moving in a white world. I was Indian but acting white. I was a traitor to my race. To cap it off, there were no models in my life of how to 'be' Indian.

But that was the plan. Cut the ties that bind people together, solder those wounds until only scars remain. The Indian Problem would go away. But it didn't. In fact, the Indian Problem became festered in me. After all, I reasoned, I was created in 'their' Caucasian image. The problem was that by making it mine, it was destroying me in the process.

The voices didn't help. Not the psychotic voices, but the voices that pecked away at my integrity, your whole-ness of being. White voices: why do you look so different from your parents? Do you speak Indian? You're adopted, I'm so sorry. Do an Indian dance for me. Do you live in a teepee? You know, all Indian girls are sluts. Indian voices: why do you talk funny? You sound white. What do you mean you don't know who your family is? You dance like a white girl. You're not Indian, so don't ever think you're one. You weren't raised on the rez, so you have no idea what it's like to be Indian.

Which explains the depression I'd fallen into in my early thirties, when I told the therapist stories of my incompetency of being a mom, or a wife, sometimes wrapping those stories in racial discord. Those were the concepts, race and gender, that therapists understood back in the day. We'd lived through the tumultuous '60s with the Black Power Movement, the Red Power movement, Women's liberation and the burning of bras. But adoption? Even if race was involved? That was a good thing. So, whatever issues I had weren't a result of my adoption.

Silence.

My depressions, the ones I went to therapists for, were really about my incompetency at being me.

***

ICWA was established in 1978 to provide a measure of protection from the ugliness. It promised us that we would be part of the weft and warp of the family and community fabric. It is important legislation and it needs to be followed; it's the law. The complication comes however, in examining the fabric that is Native society after colonization.

It is fragile, so worn in places as to be tattered, the edges frayed. There is no needle large enough to mend all these holes, and there are few people who can weave the fabric faster than it is unraveling. Therefore, the beliefs and conversations and philosophies about child placement, and 'best interests of the child' become tangled, knotted. And they should be. Any decision should take into account all the realities and possibilities, dreams and hopes that a placement and subsequent adoption brings to the table, its effect on children, its effect on families.

The problem is there aren't enough healthy families to take in all of us, children of the trauma, with more on the way. Some will still be outplaced, and in that case ICWA, as it currently stands—all or nothing—will not wipe out the feelings, the awkwardness, the storm that builds in us when we begin to question who we are, or when others force us to answer for our outside status. Those feelings can't ever be taken away; they are just part of the fabric of living in a post-colonized world.

***

Therefore, I'm left with questions.

What do I want to come from my experience? I want wars and genocide to stop so kids aren't the bargaining chips. And I want birth families to remain accessible, to the child and to the families with whom the child is placed. Every single person in this so-called adoption triad plays a crucial role in developing and supporting an individual's strength, a community's strength.

How do I support ICWA and not throw my life, or my mother(s)' under the bus? Mom just wanted a child after six miscarriages. Is that so awful? Am I supposed to feel guilty that I was the one she chose? That I was the child she was given? My birth-mom disappeared for weeks, months, at a time; leaving her eight other children with other people to raise until she reappeared back in their lives. Am I supposed to feel guilty for questioning whether she was really the best person to raise me, as she abdicated all guidance for my life, my future? By saying yes I will be invalidating the feelings of my birth-uncle, his wife, of my birth-brother, who are quick to point out the positives of this placement.

Why do I feel I am responsible in fixing this? In hiding the detritus of ideologies in contention? In mending the fabric so people can't tell how badly it is ripped?

I can't. I have my own ideologies at war. Without my placement I would never have been given a chance to be at this table, part of this important conversation about child placement. But I don't believe that dividing my family and removing them from my sight was healthy, for any of us. I needed them; they needed me. We needed us.

I can't feel guilty for what was; it was all out of my control. I can't even feel responsible for what will be; there are much larger players running the game. Therefore, I am left with a need to feel grateful; to be anything else is to invite further destruction. And I'm too tired. And I feel too old.

Therefore, I'm grateful for my birth-family and their acceptance not only of me, but of my experiences. I hope they understand that despite my absence, my re-appearance, my questions, that they are so very important to me. I am grateful for my mom, for just being a mom and not being the white mom of a little Indian girl. I hope she understood how much I needed the strength and the guidance she provided for the work that I do now. And I am grateful for my family and friends, for sticking with me on this tumultuous journey, which was almost self-destructive in nature. I hope they understand they were the net on which I rested.

And I'm grateful for my acceptance of who I am. I am a living remnant of the genocide; I am a breathing human being. I can't control who I was supposed to be. I can only control who I am now. I've raised my children to be respectful and kind and generous and productive. I live in communities where I'm accepted and find social circles where I fit in. I educate those who are ignorant of what it means to be American Indian in a post-colonized world. And I refuse to be labeled.

I no longer advocate. I no longer argue birth OR blood, real OR constructed. By doing so I realize I'd painted myself into a corner, and needed desperately to find some middle ground, because that's where I live. In between. It's not a bad place to be. It's comfortable. For me, it is the most honest niche in which I ever resided.

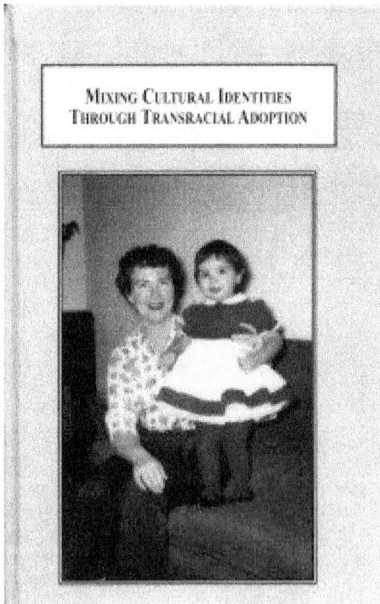

Susan Harness, an American Indian transracial adoptee, is a member of the Confederated Salish Kootenai Tribes. She is the author of *Mixing Cultural Identities Through Transracial Adoption: Outcomes of the Indian Adoption Project (1958-1967)* a book of her research that examines transracial adoption issues through the lenses of ethnic group belonging, social hierarchy, cultural capital and social memory. She has just completed her memoir *In Between: Too White to be Indian, Too Indian to be White,* which explores the transracial adoption experience through her relationships and conversations with the people it most affected:

herself, her adoptive family, her birth family and the social welfare bureaucracy that put her there. She has an M.A. in cultural anthropology and has completed an M.A. in Creative Nonfiction from Colorado State University.

17

Splitting Sickness and Genocide

Trace L Hentz (editor)

The way home is a pilgrimage of the road and an ethereal journey of the mind for adoptees—a trip of a lifetime to hallowed ground they are forced to make alone. Along the way, they must learn to comprehend the sublime, and like a good detective, be able to retrace their tracks in the sands of time. Hoping to overcome their downheartedness, they dream of solving the riddle of the maze and finding an easy passage through the fog and haze, but solving the complex mystery of life's labyrinth to find the way home without a

GPS, a roadmap, or a guide to follow is a daunting task they must undertake in solitude. —JUDITH LAND, adoptee author, *Adoption Detective*

There is no time machine to transport you back to the moment you were abandoned. You can't erase how you felt or how it feels now. Or how it controls your life. Or how it breaks your heart into a million pieces. You don't know how to stop feeling this way. You pray you'll find your family, someone like you, who gets you, who looks like you. You want to put the pieces of your life back together, but you don't know how.

These were thoughts I had writing my memoir *One Small Sacrifice*.... There are many many adoptees who feel this way yet never get to say it. No matter how much love and care we are given, the truth is—we are (and will always be) someone else's children.

Not one doctor diagnosed me with post-traumatic stress disorder, or birth trauma or my splitting sickness. Splitting sickness is what Indigenous peoples define as the survival instincts of children who have experienced great stress and trauma at a young age. It's very difficult (but not impossible) to heal. Therapists today would simply recommend drugs which would only deaden the senses, missing the whole point. As an adult adoptee I didn't want to feel more dead; I was already dead, or at least part of me was. I desperately wanted to feel alive!

I went though counseling twice. (Adoptee-centric therapy didn't exist then.)

Neither time really worked.

Instead I just shut down. Power off. Seriously. Off.

This invisible pain I describe as a dead zone, a black hole. Others call it ADOPTION FOG... **It was not visible on the skin, and I could still function and hold down a career because it's an emotional sickness, a soul injury.** (The brain is responsible for protecting us from this trauma we can't process as children.)

Years ago, I heard about another adoptee, a doctor who graduated from Harvard. He was unable to meet his natural mother before she died. He never had the chance to connect with someone in her family. His wife told me he was not able to get the information to find his birthfather, or discover that part of his ancestry and identity. (Now I would suggest DNA tests for anyone in this situation.) Regardless of this man's education and advanced medical training, this invisible pain wounded him so badly he couldn't function as a partner to his wife, show love or have a successful relationship with his children. The birth trauma was buried so deep; he really couldn't see it. His wife explained she told their therapist about his being adopted and his searching, how part of him was clearly shut down. Even after intense marriage counseling, it didn't save their marriage. Their therapist thought his early adoption trauma was too much for him to deal with; trying to work on it might kill what was left of him.

(That defines the splitting part of our condition, what we did to survive as child adoptees and how difficult it can be to heal as adults. Many don't even know that they are splitsick.) (This doctor was not American Indian to my knowledge.)

When the baby scoops of closed adoptions began, doctors apparently were not able to scientifically measure stress or trauma in the (orphaned) baby. Infants were thought to be perfectly capable to adapt and adjust to adoption and new parents. This idea has **drastically** changed in recent years. Doctors definitely note symptoms, injury and trauma in adoptees living today. There are new hospitals devoted to caring for international adoptees who develop symptoms like PTSD, reactive attachment disorder, bonding issues, mental illness and severe narcissistic injury. Scientists have also developed birth psychology, further evidence of a mom's importance to a growing baby's health and brains in the womb and months after the birth. Yes, unborn babies and newborns have intense feelings, too.

We know that much of who we are today is created in the womb. We know that mother and child are a single entity, profoundly connected physiologically, emotionally and spiritually—even through early infancy. A baby does not understand that he or she is an individual until at least nine months after birth. Losing our mother via adoption ends our life with her. It breaks our souls.

What matters is healing for many adoptees and parents of this loss.

If you have some time, google *60s Scoop* on YouTube. I do think the *shift* is happening when adoptees unite, when they tell their story, when they can finally write it or express it verbally. It's a deep act of courage.

In my humble opinion: Something awfully conflicted happens

when you are adopted like me and some of the writers in this book: one, you want to know who you are; two, you are a mystery. (Maybe you were adopted as a child and do know who you are in a remote sense of the word "know.") Some adoptees might recall or have a name, or a parents name, or a memory. Some have no idea, no clue, nothing.

The hard journey to find out who you are (based on my experience as a newborn in a closed adoption) is: intense, epic, scary, challenging, unwritten, a path with an unknown destination, a way to test your patience and courage, and it will be the hardest thing you will ever do or experience.

It's a path full of hurdles and emotional landmines.

Some days I am steel and on other days mush.

Adoptees find out that this experience is lined with people who will hate you and love you when you go searching to find your identity, your first parents, your first families. There are brick walls called sealed adoption records to break open or jump over. Emotions and secrets will blow up—yours and theirs.

Love and Hate? Yes, both. Some people don't want to be found. Some people won't like you. Some siblings won't want you around and act jealous. Adoptees do face this and some face the fact their parents are already gone when you're finally able to find them. Sadly, these are just a few of the landmines!

The general public has no idea what it feels like to be adopted and live your life as a mystery with a fake identity. Every time I look at my fake birth certificate, I laugh. It's a joke. The people who are adopted me are NOT my biological parents. But this paper says they are. It's official. It's got a seal on it. It's more a "bill of sale" and purchase agreement. I have to be this new person because these people "procured" me through adoption. I take their name and be their kid.

But I am not their kid. They don't own me.

If the general public had any idea the farce we adoptees live with and under, then all adoption laws could change faster. The laws **are** changing but very slowly. There are several years of adoption propaganda written by a billion dollar adoption industry who still need to make money. It's a BUSINESS! You will rub up against it when you see the words "Forever Family" —and the public drinks up their sweetened propaganda unknowing: They make it sound so good. It makes <u>all</u> adoption sound good.

To survive this splitting experience as an adult, I went into reunion with my dad's family when I was 38. Finding him took 16 years. Then I took on "adoption" like a college class. I got real good at chasing ghosts. I decided to find out more on orphanages, trafficking and illegal adoptions.

And then I found out even more.

The Indian Adoption Projects (including ARENA) were intended as genocide so "the government" don't dare mention or reveal that was their plan, or let the victim/survivor know, and they continue to blow smoke this ever happened. **THE STOLEN GENERATION** is called that for a reason and the governments in North America are still denying the general public the truth.

We must understand <u>this</u> history to see where we've been and where we are today to face the future united.

The affects on STOLEN GENERATIONS are <u>still</u> being felt in 2016. In Indian Country, Native adoptees are <u>still</u> called Lost Birds or Split Feathers or Lost Ones or the Stolen Generation. Many adult adoptees are <u>still</u> lost to their families and tribal nations. A lost child will remain lost with sealed adoption records <u>still</u> on the books. Today's legislators and lawmakers obviously do not know or admit or recognize the past crimes committed <u>still</u> affect us.

As I discussed in my memoir and in these anthologies, many children were stolen, literally abducted, and trafficked. This was legal since it was done with the government's approval, with programs and funding. Those social workers who drove to reservations and snatched children were **never** charged with kidnapping. Some siblings were taken but then split up in foster care and later adoptions. How did this serve the children? It didn't.

Some Native mothers were pressured in hospitals and forced to give up their newborn babies to social workers (some were nurses and nuns) trained in mental humiliation. These heartless individuals were not criminally prosecuted for coercion or harassment of these mothers.

We might ask why these Indian mothers were not offered financial assistance instead to keep and raise their own child. The adoption agencies (run by states and various religions) and social workers were *paid* to place untold numbers of Indian Children and made their careers and salaries doing it. They were not there to help Indian mothers; they were there to get the baby. This is how greed took over adoption practices. Social workers worked like Mafia to get what they needed. Long lists of people wanted to adopt and the Adoption Mafia had to fill their orders with new babies, no matter what.

EIGHT Fundamental Children's Rights:
1. Right to Life
2. Right to Education
3. Right to Food
4. Right to Health
5. Right to Water
6. **Right to Identity**
7. Right to Freedom

8. Right to Protection

http://www.humanium.org/en/child-rights/

North America's tribes lost big on the adoption battlefield: adoption brokers, missionaries and state social workers won big.

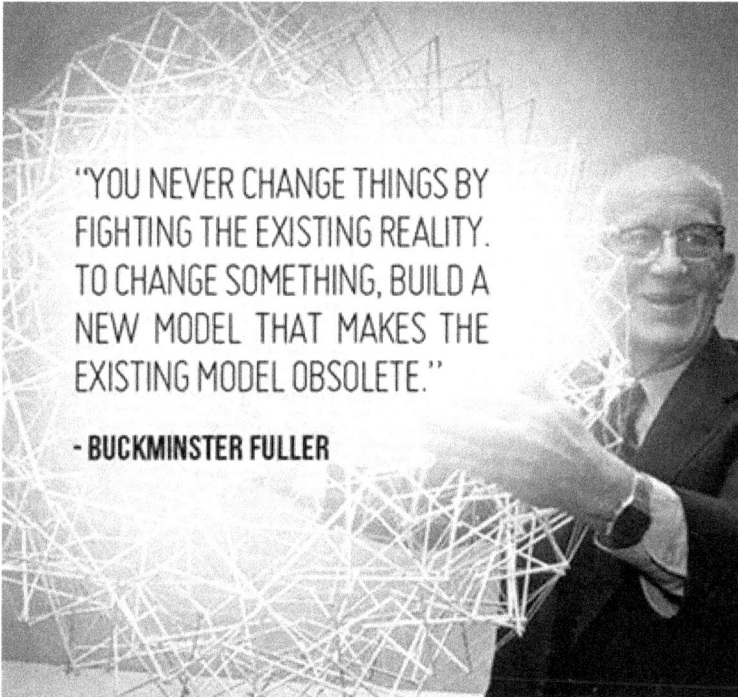

"YOU NEVER CHANGE THINGS BY FIGHTING THE EXISTING REALITY. TO CHANGE SOMETHING, BUILD A NEW MODEL THAT MAKES THE EXISTING MODEL OBSOLETE."

- BUCKMINSTER FULLER

We need a reset button: both adoption and foster care need to be reconstructed. (A better model is the SOS Villages. Every reservation needs one. LINK: http://www.sos-usa.org)

No one will deny that some Indian reservations (government concentration camps) are still places of great poverty, a condition Indigenous First Nations didn't create but a life they were forced to adapt to and survive. Even today it's a struggle but Indian people have retained many of their ceremonies, languages and cultures on these reservations and they want future generations to retain this. They want their children to live their culture, and to be able to speak their language and attend ceremony.

Finally, I ask those people who adopted us, did you have any idea what was happening to Indian people and their children? Did you know about the wholesale removals of Indian Children now described accurately as *genocide*? Did you even inquire as to why this baby or child was given up? Did you investigate or ask to meet with our birthparents? Why not? Were you aware of the adoption industry's Indian Adoption projects and programs? Most adoptive parents had no clue.

Yet these are real crimes and atrocities against Indian People yet no one involved has been charged or prosecuted?

When details of the Indian Adoption Projects were sealed and then files were closed after adoptions, a child would not have his/her name or tribal identity anymore, their birth certificate altered and falsified. Tribal membership might exist for some adoptees on paper but with secrecy and sealed files, the adult adoptee would never know or be able to find out.

It appears that was the plan.

Until adoption records are opened and Native adoptees know their family name and tribe, a crime and identity theft is still being committed.

When adoptees do return to their tribes, some find rejection. Why? Adoption changed us. We do not know our language or know our history or culture because adoption and assimilation erased it. That is not an adoptee's fault. Why is the adoptee blamed for something we didn't agree to? Why is it our fault we act WHITE?

By dividing us, these governments keep winning.

Adoptees need ceremony to heal.

Today there are non-Indians lobbying to end the Indian Child Welfare Act. This group of non-Indians feels they will be better parents to Indian children. They want no restrictions in order to adopt Indian children. Their attempt to change federal law must never happen.

It's a bloody battlefield of coercion, greed and theft of land and several generations of survivors.

—Trace (DeMeyer) Hentz, anthology editor, has been in reunion with her birthfather's side for over 20 years. Her memoir One Small Sacrifice is available on Amazon: ISBN: 978-0-557-25599-3. Trace is a mix of French Canadian, Shawnee-Cherokee, and Euro, mostly Irish.) She started the resource blog American Indian Adoptees in 2010.

18

The Indian Problem

EXCERPT:

In 1920, Duncan Campbell Scott, head of the Canadian Department of Indian Affairs said, "I want to get rid of the Indian problem. Our object is to continue until there is not a single Indian in Canada that has not been absorbed. They are a weird and waning race…ready to break out at any moment in savage dances; in wild and desperate orgies."

> "Scott saw himself as Canada's Rudyard Kipling. Perhaps he shared Kipling's vices, but not his brilliance or his irony; for Scott, natives were indeed lesser breeds without the law. His writing admired in their day now seems so much Edwardian bric-a-brac: florid, ponderous, unabashedly bigoted and racist…. Most revealing of all is one short line: 'Altruism is absent from the Indian character'. Only someone deeply ignorant, deeply prejudiced, or both could have written that." —Ronald White, *Stolen Continents*, pg. 321

1909: Dr. Peter Bryce, general medical superintendent for Indian Affairs reported to the Ministry that between 1894 to 1908 the mortality rate in western Canadian residential schools was between 35%-60%. The statistic became public in 1922. Dr. Bryce retired from his position in DIA and wrote a book, *The Story of a National Crime: Being a Record of the Health Conditions of the Indians of Canada from 1904 to 1921.* He also alleged in his book that he felt the high death rate was deliberate because healthy children had been exposed to diseases such as tuberculosis which was rampant throughout the residential school system. BOOK LINK [https://archive.org/stream/storyofnationalc00brycuoft/storyofnationalc00brycuoft_djvu.txt]

In the early 1920's another doctor, F.A. Corbett while working in Alberta, found similar startling statistics at various residential schools, including Hobbema and Sarcee. At Sarcee, only four kids from over thirty did not have tuberculosis. Moreover, with such a high illness and near death rate, the children still had to attend classes.

> "The traditional way of native education was by example, experience, and storytelling. The first principle involved was total respect

and acceptance of the one to be taught, and that learning was a continuous process from birth to death. It was total continuity without interruption. Its nature was like a fountain that gives many colors and flavors of water and that whoever chose could drink as much or as little as they wanted to whenever they wished. The teaching strictly adhered to the sacredness of life whether of humans, animals or plants." —Art Solomon, Ojibwe Elder, Residential School Survivor

SOURCE

Children were kidnapped and taken long distances from their communities in order to attend school. Once there, they were held captive, isolated from their families of origin, and forcibly stripped of their language, religion, traditions and culture. Many Native children grew up with little knowledge of their original culture. Being forced to live with no culture resulted in high suicide rates, difficulties with parenting, drug and alcohol problems, family abuse.

19

No one was talking about our experiences

Susan Devan Harness (Confederated Salish Kootenai Tribes)

Susan Devan Harness (Salish-Kootenai), author of *Mixing Cultural Identities Through Transracial Adoption: Outcomes of the Indian Adoption Project* (1958-1967) Edwin Mellen Press, NY. 2009, wrote on her blog:

Adoption Researchers, Take Note... (April 23, 2013)

As a researcher who has studied "us," I would like to weigh in. I, as an American Indian transracial adoptee, wanted to study us because no one was talking about our experiences. As transracial adoptees we were shut out and shut down as we sought to voice a counternarrative to a colonizing society. We were jeered when we tried to speak to the experiences of what it meant to be American Indian being forced to live within a world where Natives were seen as less-than. In the world we grew up in we were invisible, at best, and dead, at worst. We were feral with animalistic drives of war and sexual passion, or we were quiet, demure, compliant. We had innate musical or artistic abilities but not a lot of intellect—at least no one told us we were smart; not our parents, not our teachers. We were good storytellers and good dancers. But we didn't know how to raise our children and keep our families intact. We didn't know how to go to church and not drink on the weekends. We didn't even know our own cultures! We, as adoptees, knew the history of those thoughts; we learned the history of those thoughts, and many times we were forced to live the history of those thoughts.

Outsiders who study "us" do so from within a narrow lens, a sliver of glass that distorts what they see. Our experiences become singular, isolated, taken out of a context within a broad sweeping history of what it means to be us. They want to know how much we drink, or how often we do drugs because it then illuminates a reason for our psychological escape that doesn't include a conversation about the discomfort of a history we were made to endure. Researchers suggest a flaw—perhaps in character, perhaps it exists in our genetic code—that would explain our inability to moderate ourselves, our inability to repress our anger at families and a society that seeks to instill in us a sense of shame of being who we are. They may find we are wounded, beyond repair, because of our removal and replacement in another family. These, they argue, must be the reason for our psychiatric illnesses and our psychological lacerations.

What these research findings do *not* address is the devastation that has occurred in every single generation of American Indians over the past two hundred years as the U.S. government and religious organizations worked so assiduously to dismantle us through brutal acts of war and butchery, thousand mile forced marches over our homeland, dismemberment of our families, our children, our livelihoods, our spiritual groundings, our economy—that at one time ensured all people in the community were cared for. When these institutions took all of this away, we stood on the brink of extinction, where they told us we were bad people, and as a result put us on land that was many times not even ours to claim as territory; they said they would take care of us, and they did so, by locking us away, saying we no longer had the right to hunt or gather the way we used to, said we were such inadequate parents that our children had to go live elsewhere—and sometimes we believed them, these men of power, and we became that way. These institutions failed to provide food that they promised, or education that would allow us to thrive within the world they created, not just work for other people who lived in that created space. The anger, the frustration, the shame boiled over within these narrowly defined places of being and when we fought back the military moved against us, again and again and again. So that anger turns inward, among us, within us. We kill one another; we kill ourselves. And people shake their head and wonder how we lasted the length of time we did on this earth given our pathologic behavior.

We are tired of outsiders, those who are not adopted—transracially or otherwise—conducting studies and telling us who we are, or how we should fit neatly into some theoretical framework that is not of our making. Researchers, we are tired of filling in bubbles that don't allow for the shadowed spaces of being to be illuminated, the bubbles that indicate the black and white checkerboard of existence, the bubbles that frame us, mark us, discount us, or vilify us. Researchers, when we tell you our stories and they are misinterpreted, or even misused, we lose a sense of autonomy over those stories that we have shared so willingly, hoping you would help us understand, because we can't express the anger without consequences. We don't want to hear about how our placement was so wonderful that transracial adoption should be practiced even more. Perhaps our placement wasn't wonderful. We don't want to hear that we should just get our act together because other groups who immigrated here and were framed as drunkards and animals have done well—heck, said one friend, look at the Irish! We don't want to hear the genetic codes for inebriation can only be found in the genes of minority populations, or that mental illness runs along family lines, especially when those lines date back to the most brutal times of colonization. We want our accounts taken into consideration, made note of, discussed because perhaps we just flat out disagree with the concept of adoption altogether. Perhaps we believe it should be weighed more carefully in the minds of society, of parents, of communities or that it should cease to be a panacea for the societal illness that somehow only White people can cure.

We don't want to feel judged, de-valued, overlooked, overrun, or marginalized. We also don't want to be standardized, hypothesized, or theorized *unless you know what it feels like to be us!*

20

Adapting the Indian in the Child: The Settler Colonial Politics of Adopting Native American Children

Joshua Whitehead (Peguis First Nation Manitoba)

for my kokum, Rose Whitehead, and my father, Peter Whitehead"

In June of 2015, Manitoba became the first province to apologize to survivors of Canada's Sixties Scoop. For those unfamiliar, the Sixties Scoop refers to the removal of Indigenous children from their families, "scooping" them up, and placing them into foster homes with non-Indigenous families and/or residential/day schools. I also deploy the term Sixties Scoop with an awareness of its expansive and evolutionary nature, in that it branches beyond the sixties and moves well into the eighties; moreover, its remnants can be seen in Canada's contemporary Child and Family Services (CFS). In light of the Truth and Reconciliation Commission (TRC), Manitoba's apology was the first step towards reconciling with survivors.

Joshua, the son of a 60s Scoop adoptee

As the child of a Sixties Scoop survivor, I am interested in how adoption functions within the larger framework of North American settler colonial practices[1]. While there is quite a bit of research on the effects of adoption on adoptees and their parents, what I am interested in exploring for the purposes of this essay is the effects/affects of adoption from an intergenerational and intercommunal perspective. I ask: how does the adoption of Indigenous children from their communities and relations harm Indigeneity intergenerationally? How does the adoptive child fit into his/her/their community and moreover, how is community kinship impinged through adoptive practices? I want to place my research findings and personal experiences in tandem with the recent film, *Drunktown's Finest*, in an attempt to question how the adoption of Indigenous children away from their communities impinges entire Indigenous communities as a tool of settler colonialism.

Settler practices of adopting Native American children began largely during the Cold War and followed the popularization of American Indian boarding schools, which themselves largely began at the turn of the century. Kenn Richard, the director of Native Child and Family Services in Toronto argues that, "British colonialism has a certain process and formula, and its been applied around the world with different populations, often [I]ndigenous populations...one of the ones you hear most about is obviously the residential schools...but child welfare to a large extend picked up where residential schools left off." (DeMeyer 299). In short, adopting Indigenous children is an adaptation of previous techniques of assimilation and colonization.

Laura Briggs, in her text, *Somebody's Children: The Politics of Transracial and Transnational Adoption*, argues against Elizabeth Bartholet's popular text, *Nobody's Children*. Bartholet's text draws upon the "English common law's name for a bastard child, *filius nullius* (nobody's child, the child of no man)" as a means of structuring its argument (17). She argues that domestic U.S. policy needs to limit the amount of time that children are in foster care and push for adoption as a result. Furthermore, she argues against kinship foster care, or placing the child within their extended family, by stating that extended families are far too often unfit guardians because they too are traumatized in much the same fashion as the child. While I do not care to critique Bartholet, as Briggs brilliantly does so already in her text, I do want to draw attention to her use of the term *filius nullius*. It is here, I argue, where the specific intersections of settler adoption practices in regards to Indigenous populations are revealed. *Filius nullius*, or nobody's child, intersects with the term, *terra nullius*, or nobody's land, in a way that inextricably links native land to the body. Thus, adopting the body is a means of adopting the land. And, moreover, acquiring Native babies became a means to acquiring land to secure settler colonialism and one's own claim to their land. Thus, adoption of Native American children becomes a link in the settler colonial chain, one strongly akin to residential/boarding schools, the Indian Act, the Dawes Act, Bill C31, the Indian Relocation Act, the Indian Adoption Project, and many other formulations of national and tribal disenfranchisement.

To further extrapolate on these paradigms I draw upon Sydney Freeland's 2014 film, *Drunktown's Finest*. Freeland, a female Navajo director, released her film to critical acclaim at the Sundance Film Festival this year. The film is still unreleased on DVD and is continuing screenings in theaters throughout North America (it is available for digital purchase via iTunes in the United States). I argue that the film draws parallels between adoption of Native American children and the overall health of the Navajo community from where the adoptee is taken.

Drunktown's Finest tells the story of three characters: the hypermasculine "problem child" Luther "Sickboy" Maryboy, a (nádleehé) Two-Spirit sex worker/aspiring model named Felixia, and Nizhoni Smiles, a transethnic adoptee taken in by a white Christian family. The film revolves around and concludes with the reunion of Nizhoni and her birth grandparents, Ruth and Harmon.

In Nizhoni's introductory scene we see her writing in a dream journal. At this point in the film she is still unaware of her birth family and is called back to her Indigenous roots through dream. Nizhoni, when telling her father of her dreams is told, "Look, I wouldn't put too much stock into that." Nizhoni uses Youth Works placement as a means of travelling to the reservation. Nizhoni is given several jobs by Youth Works, one of which is Roadkill Cleanup where she is introduced to two older Navajo male characters: Copenhagen and Leroy Leroy. Nizhoni, while working with both Copenhagen and Leroy Leroy has her Nativeness questioned and disregarded. For their first clean up, Nizhoni, Copenhagen, and Leroy Leroy are called to a playground where an owl has died. Both Copenhagen and Leroy Leroy state that they must consult with their uncles in order to determine how to dispose of its body. Nizhoni, unaware of the cultural significance of the owl to Navajo culture notes, "I'm not afraid of a silly Navajo superstition" while scooping up the owl in a shovel and disposing of it in the trash bin. Afterwards, both men are upset by this and all three return to the car. In the truck we hear both men discussing her actions in Navajo. This leads to Leroy Leroy calls Nizhoni an "apple" and says that she is "red on the outside and white on the inside." Afterwards, Copenhagen asks Nizhoni in English, "You're not from here, are you?" I draw us to this scene in order to demonstrate the effects/affects of adopting Indigenous children, in that their identities become skewed, queered, and questioned by Indigenous peoples themselves. Often, Indigenous adoptees and their children must *play* Indian in order to *feel* Indian lest their Indigeneity be continually questioned and disregarded. This playing Indian can create troubling effects in regards to cultural appropriation but, after years of suffering and searching for our birth families, I must add: adoptees are not simply appropriating, they are asking for acceptance.

Nizhoni later returns to the reservation to visit her grandparents. Here she discovers that her adopted mother did not want her biological family to have contact with her and that her adopted parents denied Nizhoni a plethora of written letters, which her grandmother then gifts to her. Nizhoni, asking if her birth family agreed to the arrangement (of not having contact with he), is answered by Ruth, who states, "We did, in the beginning. They offered you a good education and a stable home. We couldn't compete with that. But the next thing we knew they shipped you off to Michigan." Thus, Nizhoni's adoptive story draws connections to the benevolent intentions of such laws as the ICWA (the Indian Child Welfare Act) which prioritizes placing Native children into Native homes though or with families that are willing to keep them within a certain proximity to their cultures. Though, as seen in the recent case of Lexi Pages[2], one's level of Nativeness comes into play and can be used to bypass the expectations set out by the ICWA through such avenues as blood quantums, Bill C31, and/or tribal disenfranchisement from the band that negate one's status within their Indigenous nation. Without such status, a family may bypass the ICWA's expectations and cut-off and/or outright restrict access to the biological family.

Nizhoni, now fully aware of her background, returns to her adopted family and questions them. Her adopted father notes that, "There were studies that said that adopted children could be traumatized if they're reintroduced into their biological families." Nizhoni's adopted mother notes, "We did this with your best interest in mind. You think I wanted you to hang out in some shack with some drunk alcoholic relatives out on the reservation?" Thus, both adopted parents draw on narratives similar to those of Bartholet, narratives of the white saviour, biological determinism, disease models and Native American's inherent predisposition to alcohol, as well as the inability for the extended family to raise their own children because they live in "Drunktown."

The film ends with all of the film's Native characters coming together for the puberty ceremony for Sick Boy's sister. It is tradition that brings them together and reinstates them into their rightful places within the Navajo community; ceremony becomes a healing and decolonizing tactic that aids all three main characters. Tradition helps Sick Boy by allowing him to participate in woodcutting for the ceremony's fire with the other men. Felixia is aided by Harmon's telling her the story of the nádleehé and the river. Finally, Nizhoni returns to the reservation on her way to college and is reunited with her grandparents while discovering that Felixia is her cousin and that Sick Boy is a "Navajo cousin." While everyone hugs, an eagle flies over the characters and Harmon informs them that it is a sign that good things are about to happen. It is through the reunion and reconnection of the adopted Indian child to her rightful community, that the community is reoriented towards a path of reconciliation and healing. It is implied that the adoption of Native children into non-Native families sits at the nexus of historical dispossession and inter-generational trauma for not only the adoptee and their family but also their kinship relations within the family.

Thus, the film draws us back to our calling for tradition and the (re)formation of a cultural nationalism that is adamant about its return to the homeland, return to the home space, and a return to the traditional in our current cultural/reconciliatory moment. The film expands definitions of reconciliation: we must also reconcile our-selves, Native-to-Native, and also decolonize what we mean by Indi-geneity. That is, I want to push us to think on an Indigeneity that is at once inclusive, intersectional, and interwoven, as a term that invites queer, non-normative, non-Status, Metis, Two-Spirit, trans, feminisms, and adoptees into its braids. I understand the anxieties around tribal membership and fraudulent Indians but I wholeheartedly advocate that we return our adopted brothers and sisters back into their rightful spaces.

Furthermore, I strongly argue that *filius nullius* and *terra nullius* are inextricably bound as assimilative and death-driven tools for settler colonialism in ways that lay claim to access to Native lands and Native bodies. Adopting the Indian in the child allows the settler to assimilate one more Indian from their lands and in doing so creates one less body to claim space in Indian country. For, as we have been made aware, we can have all the treaties we want but without a body to claim said treaties they become nullified/nullius. As Briggs has argued, practices of adopting Native American children directly followed the abandonment of residential/boarding schools. Such adoption practices, which came into fruition through forms such as the forced removal of Native American children during Canada's Sixties Scoop (and continuing today with CFS) and its parallel in the United States, the Indian Adoption Projects, exemplify the adaptation of adoption as a settler colonial tool for dispossession and disenfranchisement. Our bodies are our own, as are our lands; *terra nullius* and *filius nullius* are myths that perpetuate and naturalize settler colonialism as a savior and benefactor of Indigeneity.

Yet, I do not want to end on such a simple note as returning to tradition as a fix-all remedy. Conceptions of Native American traditionalisms and cultural nationalisms can and ought to be questioned and criticized as well. As exemplified in the film, often adoptees are disallowed re-entry into their rightful communities due in part to internalized heteropatriarchal colonialisms based on politics of recognition, blood quantums, and cultural practices. Furthermore, adoptees and their children are often not permitted entrance to cultural and/or ceremonial practices and are thus not allowed access to these knowledges which predicate their Nativeness. Adoptees and their children must "play Indian" in order to be feel and *be* Indian and this is far too often read as unfaithful and appropriative.

Thus I ask: how can we heal when ceremony isn't tailored for who we are as Indigenous adoptees? We need to go forward in our thinking of how such tools of settler colonialism, including adoption, not only dispossess us of our identities and lands but also of our modes of thinking, being, and feeling. We need to question if our current understandings of "tradition" are truly *traditional*—have we internalized colonial practices that delimit and dispossess adoptees, non-status Indians, Metis, and/or two-spirit/queer Indigenous peoples? How can we heal with tradition when tradition is an adaptation of colonization that is riddled with capitalism, heteropatriarchy, and models of the nuclear family?

I want to end with a short story of my own. In 1962, my grandmother, Rose Whitehead, was murdered in Saskatoon by a man named Steven Kozaruk. This would be the beginning of my family's bifurcation. My father and his five siblings were displaced through Child and Family Services. While I recall the stories my father tells me of his experiences, one saved newspaper clipping stands out in particular; the headline reads: "Funeral is only chance for reunion; Indians have no funds to reunite adopted-out families." In our current reconciliatory moment, I want us to also think on Native American adoptees. I want us to push for apologies (beyond Manitoba), reparations, compensation, access to original birth certificates, and more specifically, funding for kinship resurgence for families displaced through adoption: we/you/I owe this to all survivors of the Sixties Scoop and Indian Adoption Projects.

WORKS CITED

Baxter, Kent. *The Modern Age: Turn-of-the-Century American Culture and the Invention of Adolescence.* Tuscaloosa: U of Alabama P, 2011. Print.

Briggs, Laura. *Somebody's Children: The Politics of Transracial and Transnational Adoption.* Durham: Duke UP, 2012. Print.

DeMeyer, Trace A. and Patricia Cotter-Busbee. *Two Worlds: Lost Children of the Indian Adoption Projects.* Greenfield: Blue Hand Books, 2012. Print.

Jacobs, Margaret D. *A Generation Removed: The Fostering & Adoption of Indigenous Children in the Postwar Period.* Lincoln: U of Nebraska P, 2014. Print.

Klein, Christina. *Cold War Orientalism: Asia in the Middlebrow Imagination, 1945-1961.* Berkeley: U of California P, 2003. Print.

Drunktown's Finest. Dir. Sydney Freeland. Sundance Channel, 2014. Film. Trailer: https://youtu.be/Kl2Yh6YcMBU

[1] As a caveat, this essay deploys Indigeneity as a pan-Indigenous concept that applies to all of North America, while primarily focusing upon both Navajo and Plains Cree Nations as specific examples.

[2] See the Pages' family's ICWA rebuttal at http://saveourlexi.com/ (or subsequently #SaveLexi)

Joshua Whitehead is an Oji-Cree member of the Peguis First Nation in Manitoba (Treaty 1). He identifies as Two-Spirit/niizh manitoag. Joshua is currently undertaking a Ph.D. in English and Creative Writing at the University of Calgary (Treaty 7) where he focuses on Indigenous Literatures/Cultures, Critical Race Theory, Queer Theory, and Gender Studies. You can find his recent work published in Prairie Fire, CV2, EVENT Magazine, Arc Poetry Magazine, Lemon Hound, Red Rising Magazine, *and* Geez Magazine's *issue on "Decolonization".*

Confronting the Past documentary

Filmmaker and Cree adoptee Coleen Rajotte (CBC website)

I have a mission statement in life: "share stories that increase an understanding of Aboriginal peoples here and around the world."

My story began when I was adopted as a Cree child, by the Rajotte family in Winnipeg in the 1960's. From that decade until the early

1980's, thousands of Indigenous children were adopted into non-Indigenous, middle class homes. This era has become known as the "60s Scoop."

As a child, I had big dreams to become a television journalist. After high school, I attended the University of Manitoba where I was usually the only Aboriginal person in my university classes.

In the 1990's I was a television reporter for CBC's *The National* covering everything from forest fires to a big prison riot in Winnipeg, and a documentary about native street gangs.

In 1998, the CBC asked me to work on a TV current affairs program called *All My Relations*, the first in Canada to focus on Indigenous issues.

I found my biological family in 2001 and the story of my journey to discover my roots and birth family is the subject of a documentary I have been working on for years.

In 1999, I left the CBC and started making independent documentaries. My first was *Jaynelle: It's Never Easy to Escape the Past*, the story of a young aboriginal mother living for two years on social assistance. To learn more about my independent documentary work, check out www.rajottedocs.com.

In 2001, I co-founded the Winnipeg Aboriginal Film Festival with Jim Silver from the University of Winnipeg. We celebrate our 15th anniversary this year!!

In 2006, I established Vitality Television Inc. about healthy living. We have expanded the concept to "Vitality Gardening".

I have also written a screenplay based on my research around the 1960s scoop. *Concrete Indian* is the story of two brothers and their attempt to re-connect after being separated and adopted in the United States.

I have been reflecting on my life lately and I know I was meant to tell stories. As an older and wiser person, I see the full impact of colonization and I really think more has to be done to increase understanding about issues such as the intergenerational consequences of Residential Schools and the "60s Scoop."

Confronting The Past film

SIXTIES SCOOP ADOPTEES CAME TOGETHER FOR WINNIPEG ABORIGINAL FILM FESTIVAL ON NOVEMBER 24, 2015.

"It's a dark part of history, people need to recognize this," said Colleen Rajotte, WAFF director. Several Sixties Scoop adoptees took part in a day of healing as part of the Winnipeg Aboriginal Film Festival (WAFF). From the 1960s to the 80s, an estimated 20,000 Inuit, Metis and First Nations children were taken from their parents and placed with mostly white families as part of the 60s Scoop.

"This is not a well-known fact. We're really looking for the same recognition that residential school survivors have," said Colleen Rajotte, the director of the festival. "We as adoptees were sent out around the world and we never saw another brown face until we made it back home and saw our families."

Adoptees of the Scoop gathered at Thunderbird House and participated in a sharing circle, panel discussion and watched two films about adoption and children in care.

The first film the group watched was called *Miranda's Story*. The film was made by inner-city youth and chronicles a woman who has her kids taken away and adopted out to another family.

Showing that movie was meant to spark a discussion about issues currently facing the child-welfare system in Canada, Rajotte said.

Confronting the Past

The second movie, based on a true story produced by Rajotte, was called *Confronting the Past*.

"It's about three siblings from northern Manitoba. Their parents were killed in a car crash and they were sent all the way to New Orleans to a horribly abusive home," said Rajotte. "Two of them made it back, but their brother is still in a Louisiana prison."

In making the film, Rajotte went to the southern U.S. to visit and interview the brother, named Eric Orgeron, in prison.

"It really makes a point that so many of our kids have been forgotten about. We're all getting older and we really need to deal with this," she said. "Today we're really focused on, 'How can we move forward?' We need counselling, we need support, we need understanding and we need recognition."

Rajotte said there are still people out there that were adopted out and need help getting in touch with their roots and culture.

"It's a dark part of history, people need to recognize this," she said.
LINK: https://www.winnipegfilmgroup.com/films/confronting-the-past/

60s Scoop: A Hidden Generation

Missing Threads Documentary

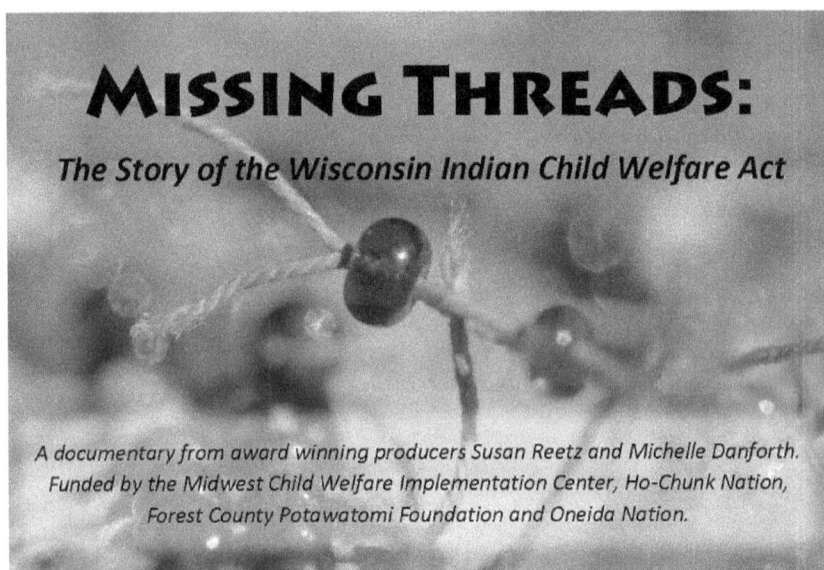

MISSING THREADS:

The Story of the Wisconsin Indian Child Welfare Act

A documentary from award winning producers Susan Reetz and Michelle Danforth. Funded by the Midwest Child Welfare Implementation Center, Ho-Chunk Nation, Forest County Potawatomi Foundation and Oneida Nation.

Film explores Native American child displacement

There is a thread that connects a child to their culture,

to their sense of self, home and belonging.

When that thread is broken or missing, the individual and the culture suffer.

Can the thread be mended? Can connection be restored?

Rucinski & Reetz Communication unveiled its video titled "Missing Threads: The Story of the Wisconsin Indian Child Welfare Act." The hour-long documentary represents nearly three years of work and "explores the connection between family, tribal culture and children, and the consequences of severing those ties," said Susan Reetz, a partner in the communication firm.

At one time, one in four American Indian children were removed from their homes and placed with white families, according to the film. The practice occurred well into the 20th century, spurring the passage of a 1978 federal law called the Indian Child Welfare Act was passed, requiring state, county and private agencies to follow specific processes when removing Indian children from their homes, according to the Wisconsin Department of Children and Families. Those processes sought to ensure that government and private agencies would make an effort to place children in Indian families. The film documents the passage of the *Wisconsin Indian Child Welfare Act*, which became law in 2009, and was designed to bolster and add to the federal law.

"It really was the deprivation of a race," said retired state senator Robert Jauch, one of the sponsors of the 2009 law. "It was unexcusable, unacceptable and avoidable."

Indian children could have been removed from their families for a variety areas, but many were "taken from their homes simply because a paternalistic state system failed to recognize traditional Indian culture and expected Indian children to conform to non-Indian ways," wrote B.J. Jones of the Dakota Plains Legal Services in a piece published by the American Bar Association.

The documentary explores how the practice of placing children in non-Indian families affected individual lives. Forest County Potawatomi Chief Judge Eugene White-Fish and Loa Porter, a Ho-Chunk Nation grandmother, both talk about their experiences of being taken from their families and placed in non-Indian households as children.

"When I was removed from my family, I was 6, maybe going on 7 years old," Porter said in the documentary interview. She remembers her sister screaming as white social workers took them away, her mother watching helplessly. "It was very, very traumatic," Porter said. "I remember it like it was yesterday."

White-Fish recounts being shuffled from family to family. "I went through six different foster homes in the time before I turned 18," he said. "I went through six different organized religions. It was very confusing because … I didn't feel like I fit."

The goal of the act is to ensure that child welfare officials, when placing American Indian foster children, do whatever is possible to place them with Indian caregivers, Reetz said. The law means that all efforts should be made to place Indian children with close family members. If that's not possible, they should be placed within their tribe, and if that's not possible, with another Indian family.

Reetz, who co-produced the documentary with Michelle Danforth, said the project was distinctive. "I feel it is an important social issue," she said.

The piece will be used to educate social workers, attorneys, judges and the general public about the issue and how the law works. It

debuted at ArtStart in Rhinelander. By late spring, the film should be widely available for free viewing on YouTube, Reetz said.
For more information, visit
http://missingthreadswicwa.blogspot.com/.
MISSING THREADS MOVIE TRAILER: https://youtu.be/U07avWbcUso

Wisconsin Indian Child Welfare Act: Legacy Legislation: 40 minutes, VIDEO: https://youtu.be/tS8WkekywV8

> Of course I was aware of the tragic circumstances in tribal communities that led to the passage of the Indian Child Welfare Act, but *Missing Threads* put faces to those tragedies for children, children who lost their families and culture by placement into foster care. These are not just any faces, but the faces of Wisconsin tribal leaders, which makes it so much more poignant, to know that the very Indian children harmed by the lack of a law to protect them were also part of the movement that successfully incorporated ICWA into Wisconsin law. The story could not be more inspiring!
> —*Merriel Kruse, Quality Review Section, Bureau of Performance Management, Division of Management Services, Wisconsin Department of Children and Families*

MAINE TRC, FIRST LIGHT, DAWNLAND
documentaries

"Imagine you're about to have a little one, the love that you have for that little one... and then imagine somebody outside of your family you don't even know making claims on your little one. They don't like the way you live and they're going to take your little one by force. Imagine what the loss is when this is not just your family, but your entire community loses its children."
—gkisedtanamoogk, Maine Truth and Reconciliation Commission member in the documentary film *First Light*

Take a look at media coverage of new film, *First Light*.

"New Film Documents Maine's Child Welfare Truth and Reconciliation Commission" -Indian Country Today Media Network

"Forced Removal of Native American Children From Parents Exposed in 13 Minutes" -WGBH (NPR Boston)

DAWNLAND: FEATURE DOCUMENTARY IN POST-PRODUCTION (2016)

When most people hear about children ripped from their families, they think of faraway places or of centuries past. The reality is it's been happening in the U.S. for centuries—and is still happening today. Native American children are more than **twice as likely** as non-Native children to be taken from their families and put into foster care, according to a 2013 study.

In Maine, a group of Native and non-Native leaders came together to acknowledge and address the abuses suffered by Native children in the hands of the child welfare system. Thanks to their commitment, the **Maine Wabanaki-State Child Welfare Truth and Reconciliation Commission** (TRC) was formed in 2012 to seek the truth and bring healing to those affected.

Dawnland is the **only** feature-length documentary to tell the inside story of this historic, **first of its kind** commission and the individuals—both Native and non-Native—who boldly and publicly came forward to share their stories of survival, guilt and loss, in order to illuminate the ongoing crisis of indigenous child removal.

The film follows key participants through the truth and reconciliation process: a survivor of foster care, a child welfare worker, a TRC commissioner, and the co-founder of the commission. Their intersecting journeys reveal buried trauma and intergroup disagreements that threaten to derail the whole process. *Dawnland* also provides essential historical context showing how these present-day conflicts are the result of 500 years of colonial domination of Native peoples. Decades of forced assimilation and misguided child welfare policy have blighted the lives of Maine's indigenous people. Can an unprecedented truth and reconciliation commission recognize centuries of abuse and begin an era of decolonization? *Dawnland* goes behind-the-scenes as this historic body redefines reconciliation, grapples with unseen truths, and transforms all involved in unexpected ways.

DIRECTORS' NOTE

Dawnland is an independent feature documentary film that uses exclusive behind-the-scenes footage to share the transformative journey of an historic body: the Maine Wabanaki-State Child Welfare Truth and Reconciliation Commission. The commission ultimately concludes that the state of Maine has been, and continues to be, engaged in "cultural genocide" against the Native people who have lived there for millennia.

Dawnland will shine a spotlight on the commission and its unprecedented response to a nationwide crisis in the United States. Today Native American children are far more likely than other children to grow up away from their families and tribes. Many of us are familiar with popular culture's portrayal of the westward expansion, Indian wars, and boarding schools. We are often taught to think that these occurred in a distant time, disconnected from people who are alive here now. The headlines hide the historical through-line from the state-funded bounty killings of Native women and children, to forced assimilation of children, to what one commissioner in Maine calls the federal government's atonement for colonial policies of dismantling tribes and families.

We released our short film *First Light* on Indigenous Peoples Day, October 2015 to begin to tell these stories to help break the silence that undermines healing. We felt we could not wait until 2017 when we plan to release *Dawnland*.

In *First Light* we tell a piece of the story of the commission and its origins. In *Dawnland* we will bring viewers inside the commission, and share testimony from those who suffered because of the child welfare system and those who upheld its policies.

FILMMAKING TEAM

Directors Adam Mazo, Ben Pender-Cudlip

Producers Adam Mazo, N. Bruce Duthu, J.D.

Executive Producer Beth Murphy

Director of Photography Ben Pender-Cudlip

Editor Kristen Salerno

Learning Director Mishy Lesser, Ed.D.

CONSULTANTS

- **Margaret D. Jacobs, Ph.D.,** University of Nebraska, author, *A Generation Removed*

- **Anne Makepeace,** director, *We Still Live Here*, *Rain in a Dry Land*

- **Alanis Obomsawin,** National Film Board of Canada, director, *Waban-aki: People from Where the Sun Rises*, *Trick or Treaty*, *Hi-Ho Mistahey!*, *Incident at Restigouche*, and others

- **George Neptune,** museum educator, Abbe Museum, Maine

ADVISORS

- **Chico Colvard,** University of Massachusetts Boston adjunct lecturer, documentary filmmaker (*A Family Affair*)

- **Donna Hicks, Ph.D.,** associate at the Weatherhead Center for International Affairs at Harvard University, author of *Dignity*

- **Dave Joseph, LICSW,** senior vice president for program, Public Conversations Project

- **Robert Koenig,** film director (*Returned*), producer, writer, and editor

- **Rebecca Lowenhaupt, Ph.D.,** assistant professor for educational leadership and higher education at Boston College

- **Dick Olsen,** strategic planner and fundraising consultant for major non-profits

First Light is the first film in a series, anchored by the feature film Dawnland (to be released in 2017), conveying the stories of pain and resilience that emerged during the Truth and Reconciliation Commission's process. It tells a piece of the story of the Commission and its origins. Dawnland will bring viewers inside the Commission and share testimony from those who suffered because of the child welfare system, along with those who upheld its policies.

> "When we tell these stories, we feel it in our bodies and our hearts. But I believe we can get to the point where it has less power over us. This was a perfect example of the readiness, that it's time." —Sandy White Hawk, TRC Commissioner.

> *First Light* and its learning resources are available for free at upstanderproject.org.

The Apology

THE APOLOGY: WORKING TOGETHER TO STRENGTHEN SUPPORTS FOR INDIAN CHILDREN AND FAMILIES: A NATIONAL PERSPECTIVE, KEYNOTE SPEECH BY SHAY BILCHIK AT THE NICWA CONFERENCE, ANCHORAGE, ALASKA, APRIL 24, 2001

"Indian people knew from the beginning that this (adoption) policy was very wrong. ... they saw this 'as the ultimate indignity that has been inflicted upon them." ... David Fanshel's 1972 Child Welfare League of American (CWLA) study of these adoptions (which only covered five years in the children's lives), concluded that while the children were doing well and the adoptive parents were delighted in almost every case, only Indians themselves could ultimately decide whether this adoption program should continue. "It is my belief," Fanshel wrote, "that only the Indian people have the right to determine whether their children can be placed in white homes." Fanshel came to this realization, as he concluded his research, because of the vigorous Indian activism that was underway in the early 1970s.

"...In the words of the Indian Child Welfare Act (ICWA), Congress endorsed the unassailable fact that 'no resource is more vital to the continued existence and integrity of Indian tribes than their children.' As you have clearly articulated, children are the future. ...While adoption was not as wholesale as the infamous Indian schools, in terms of lost heritage, it was even more absolute. I deeply regret the fact that Child Welfare League of America's (CWLA) active participation gave credibility to such a hurtful, biased, and disgraceful course of action. I also acknowledge that a CWLA representative testified against ICWA at least once, although fortunately, that testimony did not achieve its end. …As we look at these events with today's perspective, we see them as both catastrophic and unforgivable. Speaking for CWLA, I offer our sincere and deep regret for what preceded us," Bilchik said.

Going Home Star ballet: Canada's TRC Final Report

Intergenerational trauma is real and alive in communities deeply affected by residential schools. You can't attempt cultural genocide for 140 years, for seven generations—the last of these schools closing their doors in 1996—and not expect some very real fallout from that.—Author Joseph Boyden

The Final Report of Canada's Truth and Reconciliation Commission and its six-year investigation of the residential school system for Aboriginal youth and the legacy of these schools, in the summary volume, includes the history of residential schools, the legacy of that school system, and the full text of the Commission's 94 recommendations for action to address that legacy. This report lays bare a part of Canada's history that until recently was little-known to most non-Aboriginal Canadians. The Commission discusses the logic of the colonization of Canada's territories, and why and how policy and practice developed to end the existence of distinct societies of Aboriginal peoples.

Using brief excerpts from the powerful testimony heard from Survivors, this report documents the residential school system which forced children into institutions where they were forbidden to speak their language, required to discard their clothing in favour of institutional wear, given inadequate food, housed in inferior and fire-prone buildings, required to work when they should have been studying, and subjected to emotional, psychological and often physical abuse. In this setting, cruel punishments were all too common, as was sexual abuse.

More than 30,000 Survivors have been compensated financially by the Government of Canada for their experiences in residential schools, but the legacy of this experience is ongoing today. This report explains the links to high rates of Aboriginal children being taken from their families, abuse of drugs and alcohol, and high rates of suicide. The report documents the drastic decline in the presence of Aboriginal languages, even as Survivors and others work to maintain their distinctive cultures, traditions, and governance. [PAPERBACK, Publisher:Lorimer; First Edition edition (July 23, 2015), **ISBN:** 978-1459410671]

*****

Truth, Reconciliation, and Art's Ability to Heal: Joseph Boyden, author of the award-winning novels *Three Day Road* and *The Orenda,* has created a ballet inspired by a dark past that premiered October 1, 2014 performed by the Royal Winnipeg Ballet. "The idea of a ballet to commemorate the years of pain, the years of calling on survivors to come forth and allow their experiences to be recorded and archived, the years of making sure that our country never forgets, needed to end in a surge of beauty across a stage," Boyden said. "I wanted the heart of the ballet to centre on the teachings of the four directions and the traditional First Nations' colours that they represent. This would offer the story a natural structure and would allow me to create principal characters who could interact with one another." He wrote about the first Truth and Reconciliation Commission gathering back in 2010. It was called "The hurting." [http://www.macleans.ca/news/canada/the-hurting/]

A Scotiabank Giller Prize winner and author of the current bestseller The Orenda, *Joseph Boyden is one of Canada's most prominent writers.*

BALLET LINK: http://www.macleans.ca/culture/macleans-live-truth-reconciliation-and-arts-ability-to-heal/

Read more about *Going Home Star: Truth and Reconciliation* here. [http://www.macleans.ca/culture/arts/joseph-boyden-creates-a-ballet/]
And here is Boyden on what comes after the TRC. (The hard part.) http://www.macleans.ca/news/canada/first-came-truth-now-comes-the-hard-part/

Aboriginal Stolen Generations

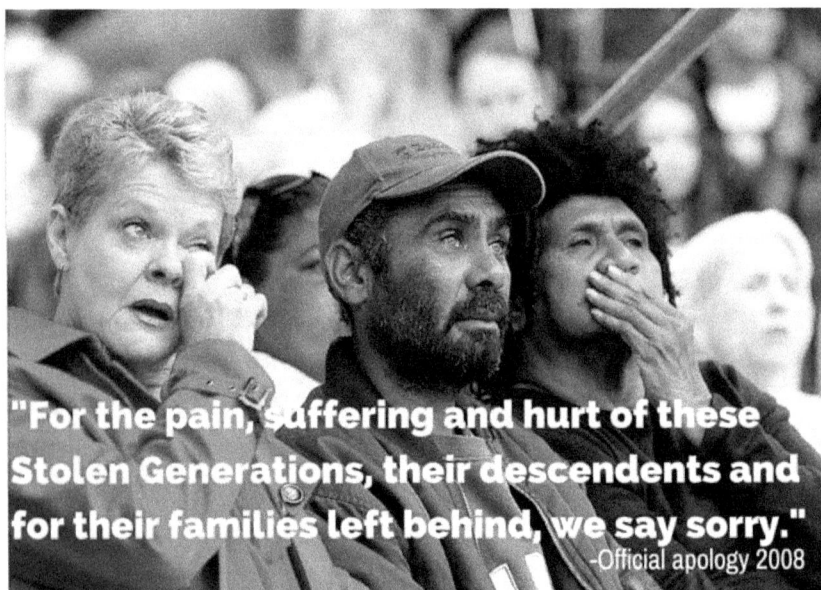

"For the pain, suffering and hurt of these Stolen Generations, their descendents and for their families left behind, we say sorry."
-Official apology 2008

Took the Children Away is a song written by Archie Roach about the terrible treatment of Aboriginal children from the Stolen Generation in Australia. Archie's lyrics for the song, Took the Children away, was made into a book with classic artwork were done by Archie's late wife Ruby Hunter. It will bring you to tears. My Australian Story: Who am I? by Anita Heiss is the story of an

Aboriginal girl named Mary who lives with the Burke's and has not seen her real mum and dad since she was taken away from them five years ago. This story is her search to find out who she is and where she belongs.

And, This is why so many of the Stolen Generation have suffered so much. The deep psychological trauma from being taken away has led so many of them to substance abuse, contact with the criminal courts and family breakdown. And the trauma is then passed onto their children.

This is a matter of urgency. We do not wish to see the emergence of another Stolen Generation.

RESPECT AND LISTEN:
HTTP://WWW.RESPECTANDLISTEN.ORG/

Helping Native Adoptees Search

Karen Vigneault
Iipay, Santa Ysabel

I was so surprised and happy to receive a gracious email from Karen over three years ago. I know many adoptees who get stuck on doing genealogy when they open their adoptions and have a name or family story that says there is INDIAN BLOOD. Once you have a name, you have to connect a parent or grandparent to a tribal roll. This has been a real problem for many adoptees.

The following interview is with Karen Vigneault-MLIS. She is an academic research librarian, genealogist and historical researcher. Karen is a member of the Iipay Nation of Santa Ysabel in California.

She has offered to help adoptees do family genealogy to be enrolled with their tribal nations. This offers hope for many of us! But remember that adoptees must do all the necessary steps to get their adoption records. She explains why this is so very important.

Karen, you have helped a few Native adoptees find their way back home. Can you share an example?

http://theacademy.sdsu.edu/TribalSTAR/services/EMailNewsletter/Archive/Sep_Oct2013/TS_Drumbeats_Sep_Oct_2013.html

Above is the link to a photo and a short article showing all that were involved in Patrick's aka Quinton's (his real name) story. It was interesting because in his case his mom was adopted as well.. but she had passed.. so we had to get both cases opened. By opening his mothers we found more info on grandmother's last name. They spelled it wrong, which meant I had to try and decipher what it possibly matched on Aleutian records. I also called Alaska and spoke to people from villages in the area asking if they ever heard the name I thought it was.. In the end we found the enrollment documents on the tribal website.. Patrick filled them out, sent out the adoption records as well.. and ultimately he was enrolled.. (We shared Patrick's story and reunion in the anthology CALLED HOME (Book 2).)

Opening records seems to be the biggest roadblock for many adoptees. How have you opened or accessed records?

I myself did not open the records. I had connections along the way and the ADOPTEE did their part in requesting info and documents… It starts with going to family court and requesting to get the records opened. Here in California we also have CILS (CA. Indian Legal Services)… which also has a form to petition to have your records opened.

http://www.calindian.org/about/cils-history

You work with another person that trains judges on these types of cases. You have opened records to get the adoptee enrolled. How did you do this?

(see above) It is important that adoptees cultivate relationships with people connected to the court system.

Have you used the Indian Child Welfare Act to petition the courts?

Yes, definitely!

Do you recommend an adoptee use someone like you and could someone get in touch with you for your help?

Yes, I think working with someone who already has the experience navigating through websites/ documents and Indian country would make the task a little easier. **I can be reached at my email: kumeyaayindian@hotmail.com**

I wish to thank Karen for this amazing offer to help adoptees in their search. She has successfully helped over 10 adoptees to my knowledge.

NOTE: The Canadian provinces all have post adoption registries. All work basically the same way. When Alberta (for example because it's the one I am most familiar with) open their registry it was advertised that the records were being opened. In the advertising it was stated how an adoptee could access the records (there was a form), it also addressed the issue of a birth parent looking for a child and how one manages a non-release. Although the system is a bit backed up (it takes a while for the information to be sent) it seems to be working quite well.

The following is from **Shea's Search Series**: The Definitive Guide to Self-Empowered Adoptee Search.

PETITIONING THE COURT TO OPEN YOUR ADOPTION FILE (FOR ADOPTEES ADOPTED IN THE UNITED STATES)

Why you should consider a petition:

Petitioning the court to open your records is something every adoptee should try. Even the most restrictive states allow the sealed adoption file to be open via court order, and petitioning the court is usually not a difficult nor terribly expensive proposition, and your odds are slightly better than winning the lottery.

As is detailed in my search series article, "Documents", the court file contains a variety of documents related to one's adoption, often including the original birth certificate. The most likely occurrence is that when petitioned, the judge will instruct that only non- or de-identified information be compiled from the file and given to you, but in a few instances, judges have been known to open the entire file. A very few judges will open files to every adoptee who asks, regardless of the reason. It pays to research how the particular judge you will be appearing in front of usually responds to petitions to open the file. Local search groups often have this information, or you can post an inquiry on an email list or Usenet newsgroup, as discussed in previous parts of this Search Series.

The details of petitioning:

Petitioning the court does not require the services of a lawyer although it can help your chances of success to use one. The first step will be determining what court has your file. You probably have already obtained this information if you followed the steps detailed in the other documents of this series. The court that has your file will be the court that finalized the adoption. In the States, this is usually a county Family court, located in the county where your adoptive parents resided at the time of your adoption. Most courts will have the proper forms for petitioning available to you on request, and you do not need to be physically present at a hearing date in order for the judge to read and respond to your petition, although appearing in person can greatly enhance your chances of success. Along with the petition, you should include the reason for your request. You may simply believe the information belongs to you, and you can state this, but the sad truth is that you are more likely to be successful if there are extenuating circumstances. If you have a medical condition that could be eased with the information or with finding your birthparents, proof and explanation of that condition should be included in your petition. If there were unusual circumstances involved in your adoption, if you know your birthparents are deceased, if you already know the identity of your birthfamily, or if your adoptive parents are deceased, you should include a statement to that effect, along with proof of your claims. However, even if you do not have any unusual circumstances, and simply want the information, you should still try a petition. As stated above, some judges will release the file to adoptees just for the asking.

Using The Indian Child Welfare Act in a petition:

The Indian Child Welfare Act is little-used, but it can be the key to a successful petition to open a sealed file if you are adopted, and are some or all Native American. The ICWA was passed in 1978 to address congressional findings that "an alarmingly high percentage of Indian families are broken up by the removal, often unwarranted, of their children from them by nontribal public and private agencies and that an alarmingly high percentage of such children are placed in non-Indian foster and adoptive homes and institutions; and….. that the States, exercising their recognized jurisdiction over Indian child custody proceedings through administrative and judicial bodies, have often failed to recognize the essential tribal relations of Indian people and the cultural and social standards prevailing in Indian communities and families."

One section of the ICWA is of particular interest to adoptees. Section 1951b states "Upon the request of the adopted Indian child over the age of eighteen, the adoptive or foster parents of an Indian child, or an Indian tribe, the Secretary shall disclose such information as may be necessary for the enrollment of an Indian child in the tribe in which the child may be eligible for enrollment or for determining any rights or benefits associated with that membership. Where the documents relating to such child contain an affidavit from the biological parent or parents requesting anonymity, the Secretary shall certify to the Indian child's tribe, where the information warrants, that the child's parentage and other circumstances of birth entitle the child to enrollment under the criteria established by such tribe."

Essentially this section directs the State to give adult adoptees of Native American heritage who request it, their birth information, so that they may enroll in their tribes. The section does allow for birthparents to file a veto, but even then the adoptee is entitled to tribal notification so that they may process their tribal rights and privileges. You can read the entire ICWA on the Web.

There are a few problem areas with using the ICWA. Many adoptees are of enough Native American blood to qualify for enrollment in their tribes, but there is nothing documented that verifies that information. Before a judge will open a file under ICWA s/he will often demand some sort of proof that the adoptee is NA at all, proof that most adoptees will simply not have. But in other instances, the agency that handled the adoption, or the court file itself, will contain notations that you, the adoptee, do have NA ancestry. If you have received non-ID from a source that states this, include a copy with your court petition. You will also need to include a copy of the ICWA in order to make the judge's work easier and predispose him/her to wanting to help you. If you have any information at all that you are even the smallest bit Native American, you should use the ICWA in your petition. Include affidavits from family members (adoptive and birth) who have told you that you have Native American blood, as well as any 'official' agency or other documents to support your claims. Remember that most tribes have small blood quantum requirements, and you should not feel guilty about using the ICWA. The intent of this law is to ensure that those of us who are entitled to tribal membership by birthright, have the *choice* to join our Native American communities.

What to Expect:

Your petition will have several possible outcomes. It can be denied outright, and you will receive nothing. Or, you might be denied identifying information, but receive censored copies of documents, or merely a summary of non-ID compiled from the documents themselves. The judge might also choose to appoint an intermediary. The intermediary will be given the file, and will conduct a search for your birthparents, usually the birthmother if you have not already found her. She will then be asked for permission to release identifying information to you. The irony is that in many cases, you still will not be given the court file or the documents contained within it, even if your birthparent(s) agrees to exchange identifying information. You will usually be required to pay for the intermediary service. In the case of the ICWA, sometimes the Court will appoint a tribal intermediary who will process your tribal enrollment in addition to seeking permission from your birthparent(s) to exchange identifying information. This is in contravention of the mandates of the Federal Act, but that does not seem to have stopped judges from doing it. Lastly, copies of parts of or your entire file might be turned over to you, unaltered.

Search Legal Notices

In most places, prospective adoptive parents are required by law to place a legal notice notifying the alleged birthfather of the impending adoption hearing. It is common practice to place these legal notices, even when the birthfather is named and has consented to the adoption, in order to erase all potential for problems later on. The attorney that represents the potential adoptors generally place these legal notices in obscure legal journals that are well known in local search circles, which is why it's a good idea to have joined a search and support group, as detailed in the post 'Initiating a Search'. Legal Notices sometimes contain absolutely no identifying information, but they *usually* will refer to you using your birthname (Baby Girl/Boy_____) and they often identify the birthfather by name as well, although sometimes he will be referred to as John Doe. The potential for payoff is enormous, however looking through the legal notices on microfilm can be an incredibly painful and time-consuming procedure. Knowing the time period when the legal notice might have been placed is tricky, and it often requires that you look through thousands of notices for several months if you are unsure when your adoption hearings were held. Knowing if the legal notice refers to you can also be tricky, unless your adoptive parents are referred to by name. Usually the name of the attorney, or the attorney's firm is named at the top of the notice, which is how you can begin narrowing down the notices.

Email me ..Trace Lara Hentz (larahentz@yahoo.com)

ICWA and the states with Existing Indian Family Exception

Trace L Hentz (editor)

As Louis La Rose (Winnebago Tribe of Nebraska) testified:

> "I think the cruelest trick that the white man has ever done to Indian children is to take them into adoption court, erase all of their records and send them off to some nebulous family ... residing in

a white community and he goes back to the reservation and he has absolutely no idea who his relatives are, and they effectively make him a non-person and I think ... they destroy him."

> ONE QUARTER OF ALL INDIAN CHILDREN WERE REMOVED FROM THEIR FAMILIES AND PLACED IN NON-INDIAN ADOPTIVE AND FOSTER HOMES OR ORPHANAGES, AS PART OF THE INDIAN ADOPTION PROJECTS... ONE STUDY FOUND THAT IN SIXTEEN STATES IN 1969, 85 PERCENT OF THE INDIAN CHILDREN WERE PLACED IN NON-INDIAN HOMES. WHERE ARE THESE CHILDREN NOW? –TRACE DEMEYER, QUOTE FROM TWO WORLDS (BOOK 1)

The Indian Child Welfare Act (ICWA) was enacted into federal law in 1978 because of the high removal rate of Indian children from their traditional homes and essentially from Indian culture as a whole. Removals devastated some tribes to near extinction levels of populations. For example, the Bureau of Indian Affairs <u>paid</u> the states to remove Indian children and to place them with non-Indian families and religious groups. The Church of Jesus Christ of Latter-day Saints (LDS Church) had an Indian Placement Program that removed Indian children from their tribes and into church members homes. By the 1970s, approximately 5,000 Indian children were living in Mormon homes.

The lack of knowledge of most social workers (and racism) also played into the high removal rates.

During congressional consideration, at the request of Native American advocacy groups, <u>huge opposition</u> was raised by several states, the Child Welfare League of America, the LDS Church, the Catholic Church, and several social welfare groups.

Despite their protests, the ICWA bill was pushed through by Representative Morris Udall of Arizona, who lobbied President Jimmy Carter to sign this historic law.

ICWA reversed this removal policy. By defining children as collective resources, essential to tribal survival, it stands as a significant exception to the rule of individualism in American law, where children's best interests are invariably assessed case by case. ICWA made the adoption of Native American children by non-native people extremely difficult by erecting significant barriers to their adoption by anyone without tribal affiliation.*

It remains a source of ongoing controversy among civil rights and children's advocates.

How the "Existing Indian Family" Exception bypasses and dismantles ICWA

In 1982, the Kansas Supreme Court held that the ICWA "was not to dictate that an illegitimate infant who has never been a member of an Indian home or culture, and probably never would be, should be removed from its primary cultural heritage and placed in an Indian environment over the express objections of its non-Indian mother."

Under the facts of the case, the court stated that the ICWA did not apply unless the child was part of an "*existing* Indian family unit."

The court denied the Kiowa Tribe of Oklahoma the right to intervene in the case, stating that the ICWA did not apply. The court also held that even if the ICWA did apply, the trial court committed no reversible error because the non-Indian mother would have objected to the transfer of the case to a tribal court and, thus, defeated the transfer. From the Kansas Supreme Court case sprang a body of jurisprudence around the "existing Indian family" exception to ICWA.

In the years following the Kansas Baby Boy L. case, approximately half of the states adopted or expanded upon this "existing Indian family" exception, despite the fact that the language appeared no where in the text of the ICWA.

Subsequent to the Kansas Baby Boy L. case, in 1989, the United States Supreme Court heard the only ICWA case that it has issued an opinion on to date in *Mississippi Band of Choctaw Indians v. Holyfield*. 490 U.S. 30 (1989)

Like the Baby Boy L. case, both parents in Holyfield consented to the voluntary termination of their parental rights and adoption of their infant by a non-Indian family. Unlike the parents in Baby Boy L., the mother in this case lived on the reservation both before and after the birth of the child off-reservation. The Supreme Court found that the child was "domiciled" on the reservation because its biological mother was domiciled on the reservation. Therefore, the exclusive jurisdiction of the tribal court under ICWA should have been invoked. The case was remanded to the tribal court for a custody determination three years after the child had been placed with non-Indian adoptive parents. Noting the potential disruption in the child's life, the Supreme Court noted that any potential harm could have been avoided if the parents and state court had not wrongfully denied the tribe its rights under ICWA.

While the Supreme Court did not consider the "existing Indian family" exception, some sources cite Holyfield as an implicit rejection of the exception.

Other sources have noted that the Holyfield case is relied upon as support for both sides of the debate over the "existing Indian family" exception:

> "Surprisingly, Holyfield has been relied upon by courts and parties both to support and reject the existing Indian family exception, which has been invoked in proceedings involving Indian children and families who are living off the reservation and who are, therefore, subject to state court jurisdiction concurrent with that of the tribal court."

As of 2010, Alabama, Indiana, Kentucky, Louisiana, Missouri, and Tennessee still use the "existing Indian family" exception. Alabama and Indiana have limited its application by further court decisions. Nineteen states have rejected the doctrine, either by court decision or statute, including Kansas, where the Kansas Supreme Court expressly overturned the Baby L. decision in In re A.J.S., stating:

> "Given all of the foregoing, we hereby overrule Baby Boy L., (citation omitted), and abandon its existing Indian family doctrine. Indian heritage and the treatment of it has a unique history in United States law. A.J.S. has both Indian and non-Indian heritage, and courts are right to resist essentializing any ethnic or racial group. However, ICWA's overall design, including its "good cause" threshold in 25 U.S.C. 1915, ensures that all interests—those of both natural parents, the tribe, the child, and the prospective adoptive parents—are appropriately considered and safeguarded. ICWA applies to this state court child custody proceeding involving A.J.S., and the Cherokee Nation must be permitted to intervene."

CRITICISMS

Some critics have complained that the existing Indian family exception requires the state court to determine what it means to be an Indian child or an Indian family, by applying tests to determine the "Indian-ness" of the child. One such test involved evaluating if the child lived "in an actual Indian dwelling," apparently thinking of a teepee, hogan, or pueblo." Another work notes that "state courts have taken it upon themselves to determine individuals' relationship with their tribes by examining such contacts as subscription to a tribal newsletter." [Source: **Wikipedia**]

In her 1997 testimony before the Joint Hearing of the House Resources Committee and the Senate Committee on Indian Affairs, Assistant Secretary of the Interior Ada Deer (Menominee Indian Tribe of Wisconsin) stated:

"...we want to express our grave concern that the objectives of the ICWA continue to be frustrated by State court created judicial exceptions to the ICWA. We are concerned that State court judges who have created the "existing Indian family exception" are delving into the sensitive and complicated areas of Indian cultural values, customs and practices which under existing law have been left exclusively to the judgment of Indian tribes... We oppose any legislative recognition of the concept."

Editor's Note: 566 tribes are federally recognized by the BIA in 2016. These numerous state courts in the USA do not understand that 80 percent of Native Americans do NOT live on reservations, primarily because of few jobs or a stable economy. Racism and ignorance is apparent with these existing Indian Family exceptions. In 2008, a total of 62 Native American tribes had been recognized by states, not the BIA. It's been said over 200 tribes are petitioning the BIA for federal recognition and some have been waiting over 30 years. Native Americans do intermarry and despite having a non-Indian mother or father, their child is still considered a tribal member and sovereign under the ICWA.

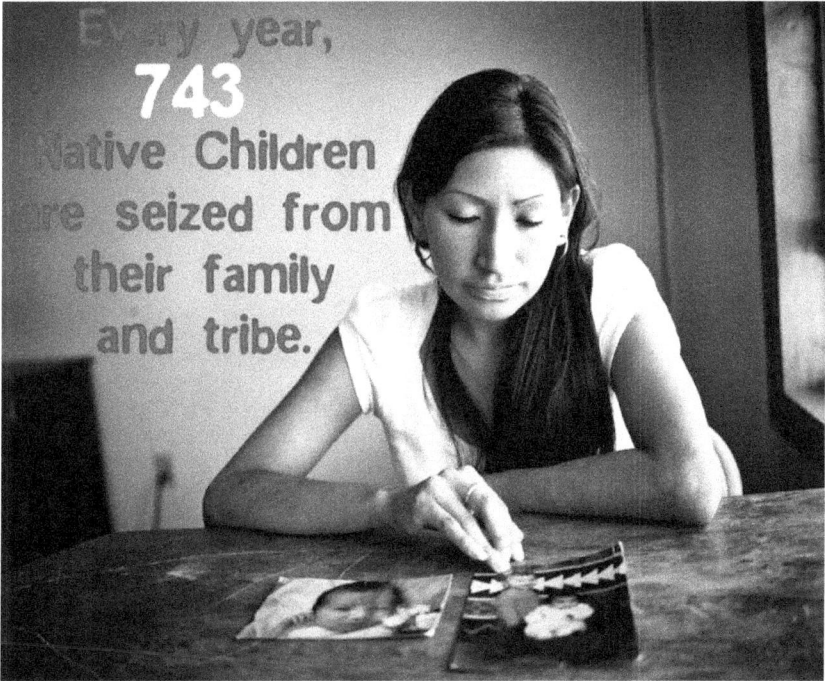

Help the Lakota Law Project investigate South Dakota's foster care system! SIGN THE ?PETITION: lakota.cc/16I9p4D

*In the United States, persons of Native American descent occupy a unique legal position. On the one hand, they are U.S. citizens and are entitled to the same legal rights and protections under the Constitution that all other U.S. citizens enjoy. On the other hand, they are members of self-governing tribes whose existence far predates the arrival of Europeans on American shores. They are the descendants of peoples who had their own inherent rights—rights that required

no validation or legitimation from the newcomers who found their way onto their soil. [West's Encyclopedia of American Law, edition 2. Copyright 2008 The Gale Group, Inc. All rights reserved.]

Remnants

We are the remnants of great warrior nations

    We are living reminders of bad dreams and broken treaties

    We are descendants of a people robbed of ancestral lands

    We are remnants because the government wanted to destroy us all

    We are survivors after they broke up our families to break our spirit and take our land

    We are still here after decades of battle and death

    We are still sovereign

    We are still Indian even if we were taken as children and assimilated

    We lost our mothers and they lost us

    We were little children abducted to boarding school and to white families who adopted us…

    We live across America and Canada now

    We wait to be repatriated

    We wait for an apology that may never come

    We wait for our naming ceremony

    We wait to be recognized and welcomed back as tribal citizens*

    We will reclaim our language and ceremonies

    We have been given no other choice

We will wait and wait longer
We are remnants and descendants of the last great warriors
We still wait.

Trace Hentz also uses the penname Laramie Harlow. *Remnants* is from her second chapbook BECOMING. (ISBN: 978-0692285138)

*Adoptees have shared what they heard: "Now we're too white, too loud, too brainwashed, too educated, ask too much, expect too much. You're not Indian anymore, get it?"

An elder told me to pray a few Tsalgi words often. "You didn't lose your right or power to do that," he said. Ea Nigada Qusdi Idadadvhn. Translated: We are all related.

Bibliography

MEMOIRS:

Looking for Lost Bird: A Jewish Woman Discovers Her Navajo Roots, Yvette Melanson (Navajo), Harper Perennial; Reprint edition (January 5, 2000) **ISBN:** 978-0380795531

Hidden Heritage: The Story of Paul LaRoche (Lower Brule) – Babara Marshak, Beaver's Pond Press; 3rd edition (June 30, 2005) **ISBN:** 978-1592981359

Cricket: Secret Child of a Sixties Supermodel, Memoir, Suzie Fedorko (Ojibwe), Outskirts Press (November 1, 2012), **ISBN:** 978-1432795007

One Small Sacrifice: A Memoir, Lost Children of the Indian Adoption Projects, Trace DeMeyer (French Canadian-Shawnee-Cherokee), Blue Hand Books; (2009) 2nd edition (April 26, 2012) **ISBN:** 978-061558215X

Lost Bird of Wounded Knee: Spirit of the Lakota, Renee Sansom Flood, Scribner; second printing edition (May 24, 2014) **ISBN:** 978-1476790752

Pipestone: My Life in an Indian Boarding School, Adam Fortunate Eagle, University of Oklahoma Press; First Edition edition (March 19, 2010) **ISBN:** 978-080614114X

Mixing Cultural Identities through Transracial Adoption: Outcomes of the Indian Adoption Project (1958-1967), Susan Devan Harness (Salish-Kootenai), The Edwin Mellen Press (2009) **ISBN:** 978-0779914325 [Forcibly adopted American Indians torn between cultures, feature story,

Denver Post: http://www.denverpost.com/ci_13887007] Susan has just completed her memoir *In Between: Too White to be Indian, Too Indian to be White (2016) (to be published soon.)*

Adoptionland: From Orphans to Activists, Edited by Janine Myung Ja, Michael Allen Potter, and Allen L. Vance, (September 12, 2014). Trace (DeMeyer) Hentz contributed. ISBN: 9781500957940

RECOMMENDED READING:

Lost Birds: Four adopted women seek out their Native American roots, Produced by Danielle J. Powell, Joshua J. Friedman and Cassandra Herrman for Fault Lines on AL JAZEERA America: https://ajfaultlines.atavist.com/lostbirds#chapter-82819

Accounting for the 60s Scoop – by Colleen Rajotte (2012)
– My adoption story as an Indian child starts at the old Grace Hospital in Winnipeg in 1968. That's the year I was legally adopted by a white, middle-class family. Like 20,000 other aboriginal children taken from their families in the 1960s, '70s and early '80s, I have been on a life-long journey to reconnect with my family and culture and to figure out how to fit into both of these worlds. LINK:
http://www.winnipegfreepress.com

SOMEBODY'S CHILDREN: The Politics of Transracial and Transnational Adoption by Laura Briggs. Duke University Press Books; (March 7, 2012) **ISBN:** 978-0822351610

Karen Tani, *The Long History of the Indian Child Welfare Act*, JOTWELL (November 5, 2013) (reviewing Margaret D. Jacobs, *Remembering the "Forgotten Child": The American Indian Child Welfare Crisis of the 1960s and 1970s*, 37 **American Indian Quarterly** 136 (Winter/Spring 2013)), http://legalhist.jotwell.com/the-long-history-of-the-indian-child-welfare-act/.

Margaret D. Jacobs, *Remembering the "Forgotten Child": The American Indian Child Welfare Crisis of the 1960s and 1970s*, 37 **American Indian Quarterly** 136 (Winter/Spring 2013).

March 14, 1966.

ADOPTIONS OF INDIAN CHILDREN INCREASE

One little, two little, three little Indians--and 206 more--are brightening the homes and lives of 172 American families, mostly non-Indians, who have taken the Indian waifs as their own.

Once the success of the boarding schools was called into question, the dominant belief was that Native children were better off raised in white homes. To that end, in 1958, the Bureau of Indian Affairs created the Indian Adoption Project, administered by the Child Welfare League of America, to promote adoption of Native children from sixteen western states by white adoptive families in the East.

In 1966 the BIA announced in a press release that adoptions of Indian children through the Indian Adoption Project, with help

from the Child Welfare League of America, were increasing and
boasted that"little Indians" were brightening the homes and lives
many American families, mostly non-Indians. The children
ranged in age from newborn to 11 years.

Alfred, G. (1999). *Peace, power and righteousness: an indigenous manifesto.*
Toronto, ON: Oxford University Press.

Battiste, M. & Henderson, J. (2000). *Protecting indigenous knowledge and heritage: a global challenge.* Saskatoon, SK: Purich.

Haig-Brown, C. (1988). *Resistance and renewal: surviving the Indian residential school.* Vancouver, BC: Tillacum.

Harper, M. (1993). *"Mush-hole" memories of a residential school.* Toronto, ON: Sister Vision.

Meyer, M.A. (2001). Acultural assumptions of empiricism: a Native Hawaiian critique. *The Canadian Journal of Native Education,* 25(2), 188-198.

Meyer, M.A. (2005). Remembering our future: Hawaiian epistemology and the specifics of universality. *International Indigenous Journal of Entrepreneurship, Advancement, Strategy and Education.* 49-55.

Moore, MariJo (Ed.). (2003). *Genocide of the mind: new Native American writing.* New York, NY: Thunder's Mouth.

National Council of Juvenile and Family Court Judges, *Disproportionality Rates for Children of Color in Foster Care (Fiscal Year 2013).*

Palmiste, Claire, "From the Indian Adoption Project to the Indian Child Welfare Act: the resistance of Native American communities," *Indigenous Policy Journal Vol. XXII, No. 1 (Summer 2011).*

Sullivan, L., & Walters, A. (October 25, 2011). Native Foster Care: Lost Children, Shattered Families. National Public Radio. Available online at http://www.npr.org/2011/10/25/141672992/native-foster-care-lost-children-shattered-families and http://www.npr.org/2011/10/25/

141475618/disproportionality-rates-of-native-american-children-in-foster-care.

Lost Daughters: Writing Adoption from a Place of Empowerment & Peace, Edited by Amanda H.L. Transue-Woolston, Julie Stromberg, Karen Pickell, and Jennifer Anastasi, CQT Media And Publishing (March 22, 2014), **ISBN:** 978-0988585847 (Trace contributed Mending the Hoop.)

Puxley, Chinta, The Canadian Press, Residential School Survivors Reporting Hearing Loss, Broken Bones, Respiratory Illnesses: LINK: http://www.huffingtonpost.ca/2014/07/27/residential-school-survivors

Hidden Generations/60s Scoop Blog: https://ahiddengeneration.com/

The Colonial Problem: An Indigenous Perspective on Crime and Injustice in Canada, Lisa Monchalin, University of Toronto Press, Higher Education Division (March 8, 2016) **ISBN:** 978-1442606623

READ: ICWA [https://www.law.cornell.edu/uscode/text/25/chapter-21] has not been amended, updated, or changed. **Ever.** The same language that Congress passed in 1978 is the

same language in effect today. MORE:
https://turtletalk.wordpress.com/2016/03/29/icwa-case-
updates-and-legal-clarifications/

American Indian Adoptees blog has received over a half a
million visits: www.splitfeathers.blogspot.com

INDIAN ADOPTION PROJECTS:

Called Home, Book 2: Lost Children of the Indian Adoption Projects Paper-
    back, Blue Hand Books; First edition (June 27, 2014) **ISBN:**
    978-0692245880

Two Worlds, Book 1: Lost Children of the Indian Adoption Projects (60s
    Scoop), Blue Hand Books; First edition (September 25, 2012) **ISBN:**
    978-1479318280

The Stolen *Children* of Maine: Native Wabanaki Seek Truth
    ...*[http://inthesetimes.com/rural-america/entry/18201/stolen-children-
    maine-native-wabanaki-truth-reconciliation-genocide]*

–JACOBS, MARGARET D., A GENERATION
REMOVED: THE FOSTERING AND ADOPTION
OF INDIGENOUS CHILDREN IN THE POSTWAR
WORLD, MARGARET D. JACOBS, UNIVERSITY
OF NEBRASKA PRESS; FIRST EDITION, FIRST
PRINTING EDITION (SEPTEMBER 1, 2014)
ISBN: 978-0803255365

–JACOBS, WHITE MOTHER TO A DARK RACE:

SETTLER COLONIALISM, MATERNALISM, AND
THE REMOVAL OF INDIGENOUS CHILDREN IN
THE AMERICAN WEST AND AUSTRALIA,
1880-1940. UNIVERSITY OF NEBRASKA PRESS
(MARCH 1, 2011) ISBN: 978-0803235168

Intergenerational Trauma: The Ghosts of Times Past. Thomas L Hodge
    (Author) (February 3, 2016) **ISBN:** 978-1523865581

The Indian Child Welfare Act Handbook: A Legal Guide to the Custody
and Adoption of Native American, B. J. Jones, American Bar Association; 2nd edition (June 23, 2008) ISBN: 978-1590318584

Facing the Future: The Indian Child Welfare Act at 30 (American Indian
Studies), Matthew L. M. Fletcher, American Indian Studies, Michigan
State University Press (December 1, 2009) **ISBN:** 978-0870138607

Children, Tribes, and States: Adoption and Custody Conflicts
Over American Indian Children, Barbara Ann Atwood,
Carolina Academic Press (April 30, 2010) **ISBN:**
978-1594605222

Bilchik, S. (2001, April 24). [Keynote address]. Speech presented at
the 19th Annual Protecting our Children Conference, Anchorage,
AK.

Child Welfare League of America. (1960, April). Indian Adoption Project.
    New York: Author.

Demer, L. (2001, May). Native receive apology for 1950s racial adoptions.
    Pathways Practice Digest, 1-2.

Lyslo, A. (1962, December). Suggested criteria to evaluate families to adopt American Indian children through Indian Adoption Project. New York: Child Welfare League of America.

Lyslo, A. (1964). The Indian Adoption Project: An appeal to catholic agencies to participate. Catholic Charities Review, 48(5), 12-16.

Lyslo, A. (1967, March). 1966 year end summary of the Indian Adoption Project. New York: Child Welfare League of America.

Lyslo, A. (1967). Adoptive placement of Indian children. Catholic Charities Review, 51(2), 23-25.

Lyslo, A. (1968, April). The Indian Adoption Project – 1958 through 1967: Report of its accomplishments, evaluation and recommendations for adoption services to Indian children. New York: Child Welfare League of America.

Laura Briggs, "Mother, Child, Race, Nation: The Visual Iconography of Rescue and the Politics of Transnational and Transracial Adoption," *Gender & History* 15 (2003):179-200.

Sherman Alexie, *Indian Killer* (New York: Warner Books, 1996).

Robert Benson, ed., *Children of the Dragonfly: Native American Voices on Child Custody and Education* (Tucson: University of Arizona Press, 2001).

Joan Heifetz Hollinger, "Beyond the Best Interests of the Tribe: The Indian Child Welfare Act and the Adoption of Indian Children," *University of Detroit Law Review* 66 (1989):451-501.

Marilyn Irvin Holt, *Indian Orphanages* (Lawrence: University Press of Kansas, 2001).

Sondra Jones, "Redeeming the Indian: The Enslavement of Indian Children in New Mexico and Utah," *Utah Historical Quarterly* 67 (1999):220-241.

Barbara Kingsolver, *Pigs in Heaven* (New York: Harper Perennial, 1993).

Arnold Lyslo, "Adoptive Placement of American Indian Children With Non-Indian Families," in *Readings in Adoption*, ed. I. Evelyn Smith (New York: Philosophical Library, 1963), 231-236.

Steven Unger, ed., *The Destruction of American Indian Families* (New York: Association on American Indian Affairs, 1977).

MORE ADOPTION PROJECTS:

The Rainbow Project: Pennsylvania, Pittsburgh Press, August 30, 1984.

The Adoption Resource Exchange of North America (ARENA), founded in 1966, was the immediate successor to the Indian Adoption Project. ARENA was the first national adoption resource exchange devoted to finding homes for hard-to-place children. It continued the practice of placing Native American children with white adoptive parents for a number of years in the early 1970s. The (ARENA) exchange registered more than 400 families and 200 children across the country in the last two years, and assisted in placing more than 100 Native American children. However, about 200 of the registered families are waiting for home studies.

FMI: Anthology *CALLED HOME: Lost Children of the Indian Adoption Projects (2014) ARENA (Adoption Resource Exchange of North America) continues and expands after the IAP. States create their own programs, like New York's OUR INDIAN PROGRAM. Churches like the Mormons and Catholics run their own programs.*

Our Indian Program, New York state Louise Wise Services, "Our Indian Program," 1960 (see *One Small Sacrifice: A Memoir*)

Operation Papoose: Using adoption to disrupt Indian families, North American Indian children are placed in orphanages, foster homes or with non-Indian parents. The American government creates the Indian Adoption Project

(IAP) run by Arnold Lyslo in New York. Lyslo travels to different states to convince the social workers to line up white parents for the flood of Indian kids being snatched up for adoption. An article ran in the MIAMI NEWS newspaper about OPERATION PAPOOSE [June 25, 1964]

Indian Adoption Project Evaluation, 1958 through 1967 (Source: http://pages.uoregon.edu/adoption/archive/LysloIAP.htm)

Arnold Lyslo, "Suggested Criteria to Evaluate Families to Adopt American Indian Children Through the Indian Adoption Project," 1962 [http://pages.uoregon.edu/adoption/archive/LysloSCTEF.htm]

"The Indian Adoption Project—1958 through 1967—Report of Its Accomplishments, Evaluation and Recommendations for Adoption Services to Indian Children," pp. 1, 6, 8, Child Welfare League of America Papers, Box 16, Folder 2, Social Welfare History Archives, University of Minnesota.

STUDY: David Fanshel, *Far From the Reservation,* 1972

Indian Child Welfare Act, 1978: http://pages.uoregon.edu/adoption/archive/ICWAexcerpt.htm

Study by Jeannine Carriere (First Nations) (2007) Promising practice for maintaining identities in First Nation Adoption,

Complete text here: http://www.olc.edu/local_links/
socialwork/OnlineLibrary/Carriere%20(2007)

ABOUT THE ARTIST:
Terry Niska Watson

This illustration I painted years ago when I was in a very dark place in my life. This is a painting of a subject matter that has always drawn my interest that is the Native life and the beauty of tradition, family and nature. As my sister, Elizabeth Blake, said about this painting that still hangs on my wall, "the most interesting part is that the face is not visible. That is how it is when you do not know your birth family."

...My father is more of a mystery, but from what I do know, he was an enrolled member of the White Earth Chippewa tribe of Minnesota, Mississippi band. He was raised by a paternal great aunt and her husband, who I assume had the Murray surname. Apparently his mother, Josephine (Rice) Murray/ Maydwayausung died young and his father, George Murray could not take care of him. He had a brother, whose name I do not know either, but I am investigating every lead I can get.

My father worked in the CCC camps and then joined the Army in 1950 and served until 1954, where he received a Korean Service ribbon, United Nations Service medal, Army of Occupation (Germany), Defense service medal and a Meritorious Unit Commendation. He was a paratrooper part of the time and he reenlisted in 1955, according to adoption records, but no military service records reflect this. He also received monetary compensation as a disabled veteran and this carried over into our lives as adoptees, as we got some financial help with school for a few short years. It is unfortunate that apparently, my birth father became an alcoholic, what led up to this, I will never know.

I have gleaned some information from the Children's Home Society paper-work which states "the birthfather reluctantly concluded that he and the birthmother could not care for their children and that the best plan for them would be commitment as wards of the state. He was most unwilling to think in terms of adoption and could not discuss this rationally. He became depressed and denied that the problem had to be solved that way." The same paperwork goes on to elaborate, "It appeared to the caseworker that the birthfather could accept guardianship just as he had the foster home placement simply because he recognized that his children needed care.

But he wanted to believe that he could still call them his own and that he was their father." I find this very sad and disheartening to think that my father tried to be a father and was told he couldn't. Because of my birthmother's confirmed schizophrenia and inability to care for us, he lost his will and his right to father his own children—was this what made him dive deeper into the drink? One can never be sure and this bothers me: *I am so sorry, Father.*

Terry Niska Watson (White Earth Ojibwe) contributed her reunion story in the anthology CALLED HOME (Book 2) Lost Children of the Indian Adoption Projects.

ABOUT THE AUTHOR

Trace (DeMeyer) Lara Hentz, Stolen Generations anthology editor, has been in reunion with her birthfather's side for over 20 years.

Poet, mosaic artist, author, professional blogger, this award-winning journalist is former editor of the *Pequot Times* in Connecticut and editor/co-founder of *Ojibwe Akiing* in Wisconsin. Her writing, interviews and poetry has been published in newspapers and journals in the USA, Canada and Europe. Her first book "*One Small Sacrifice: A Memoir, Lost Children of the Indian Adoption Projects*," broke new ground in 2009 and a second edition was published in 2012. (It's still in the Top 100 Native biographies on Amazon.)

Trace occasionally writes book reviews and features/interviews for News from Indian Country, a national independent native newspaper, and Whisper and Thunder online magazine. DeMeyer's chapter on Sac and Fox Olympian Jim Thorpe won critical praise in the 2001 book *Olympics at the Millennium* (published by Rutgers Press). Her poetry was published in the spring 2009 edition of Yellow Medicine

Review; and she has poetry in the Foothills Press book, *I Was Indian Before It Was Cool*, edited by Susan Deer Cloud.

In November 2011, Trace founded Blue Hand Books as a publishing collective for other Native authors [www.bluehandbooks.org] publishing 15 titles in 5 years, most notably the stunning debuts *Pointing with Lips* by Dana Lone Hill (Lakota) and *Sweetgrass Burning: Stories from the Rez* by Santa Fe author Barbara Robidoux (Eastern Cherokee).

Two non-fiction anthologies Trace co-authored and edited are "Two Worlds" and "Called Home" (Books 1 and 2: Lost Children of the Indian Adoption Projects) with Patricia Busbee (Cherokee) that featured American Indian adoptees narratives and history. With MariJo Moore (Cherokee), they published an anthology "*Unraveling the Spreading Cloth of Time: Indigenous Thoughts Concerning the Universe*" in 2013. She contributed the chapter *Mending The Hoop* in the Lost Daughters anthology. LINK

"*Sleeps with Knives*" and "*Becoming*" (prose poems and short stories) Trace published using the pen-name Laramie Harlow (using a paternal family last name).

She's contributed to many acclaimed books on adoption and was a presenter and panelist at the American Indian Workshop in Europe in 2005 and has given book presentations at numerous universities in the USA and Canada. In 2014, Trace was executive producer of the Nightwolf Radio Program in Wash. DC. Currently she's teaching blogging and social media at Greenfield Community College. A mix of American Indian (Shawnee-Cherokee) and French Canadian-Irish, Trace is a graduate of the University of Wisconsin-Superior with a Bachelor of Fine Arts, and lives at the foot of the Berkshires in western Massachusetts with her husband Herb.

Please Tell Your Friends

WEBSITE/BLOG:
WWW.BLUEHANDBOOKS.ORG

FACEBOOK PAGE:
HTTPS://WWW.FACEBOOK.COM/
BLUE-HAND-BOOKS

TWITTER:@BLUEHANDBOOKS

EMAIL:
BLUEHANDCOLLECTIVE@GMAIL.COM

BLUE HAND BOOKS
Loki: God of Mischief
THEN IT HIT ME
BECOMING
Laramie Harlow
CARLOMAGNO
Two Worlds
Narragansett Poetry
John Christian Hopkins
one small Sacrifice
Called Home
TWO GUNS
remedies
PATRICIA COTTER BUSBEE
MADE IN THE USA
POINTING WITH LIPS
Writer on the Storm
John Christian Hopkins
Sleeps with Knives
OJIBWE HUNTER
WWW.BLUEHANDBOOKS.ORG